Edward McInnes

»Ein ungeheures Theater«
The Drama of the
Sturm und Drang

Verlag Peter Lang
Frankfurt am Main · Bern · New York · Paris

CIP-Kurztitelaufnahme der Deutschen Bibliothek

McInnes, Edward:

"Ein ungeheures Theater" : the drama of the Sturm und
Drang / Edward McInnes. — Frankfurt am Main ; Bern ;
New York ; Paris : Lang, 1987.
(Studien zur deutschen Literatur des 19. [neunzehnten]
und 20. Jahrhunderts ; Bd. 3)
ISBN 3-8204-9852-4
NE: GT

ISSN 0930-2166
ISBN 3-8204-9852-4

Druck und Bindung: Weihert-Druck GmbH, Darmstadt

'Ein ungeheures Theater'

The Drama of the Sturm und Drang

Studien zur Deutschen Literatur des 19. und 20. Jahrhunderts

Herausgegeben von Dieter Kafitz (Mainz)

Band 3

Verlag Peter Lang

Frankfurt am Main · Bern · New York · Paris

To my Mother and the Memory

of my Father.

CONTENTS

Acknowledgements

I am deeply indebted to the British Academy for a research grant in Autumn 1982, which allowed me to carry out some of the basic research for this volume at universities in West Germany. Chapter Two of this study is a modified English version of an essay *Politik, Moralität und Geschichte in 'Götz von Berlichingen'*, which appeared in the Goethe-Sonderheft of the Zeitschrift für deutsche Philosophie, 103, 1984. I have also used in different parts of the book material from a lecture *'Mercier and the Drama of the Sturm und Drang'* which appeared in Proceedings of the English Goethe Society, 54, 1984. I am grateful to the editors of both journals for permission to re-print.

I would also like to express my thanks to Professor Dr. Dieter Kafitz (Mainz) for his generous encouragement and help, and to Mrs Catherine Ready for the care, patience and constant good humour with which she typed the manuscript.

The University of Hull,

England.

9

INTRODUCTION

The Sturm und Drang was a short-lived and closely circumscribed movement. Literary historians have never had any trouble in saying precisely where and when it developed and who its main participants and adherents were. They have also found it just as easy to determine which of its relatively few works had a powerful impact on the individual members of the movement and on the wider world of its time. Yet despite all these clear-cut certainties commentators over the years have disagreed persistently and profoundly about the character ot the Sturm und Drang, its determining aims and aspirations, and its place in the development of German literature. Few movements, as brief and limited as this one, can ever have been subjected to such a variety of critical description and assessments.

In the second half of the 19th-century critics like Scherer and Erich Schmidt were concerned to see the Sturm und Drang first and foremost as the emanation of the creative genius of the young Goethe and thus sought to present it as an early, preparatory phase in the development of German classicism.[1] In the early part of our own century, however, this view seemed to fall out of favour. At this point critics were concerned rather to stress the force of the irrational in the outlook of the Stürmer und Dränger, and sought to interpret the movement as a 'Präromantik', a powerful, if brief, forerunner of German romanticism.[2] This view was rooted in the conviction that the Sturm und Drang arose out of a violent reaction against the rationalism of the Enlightenment – a conviction which continued largely to dominate critical approaches throughout the inter-war years. This view too was soon to come under increasingly serious challenge. Under the influence of Marxist critics like Lukács, Stolpe and Braemer more and more commentators in the past thirty years or so have attempted to show that the Sturm und Drang represents not so much a rejection of the Enlightenment as a new phase in its development, not so much its negation as its radical, questioning extension.[3] The controversy about the Sturm und

11

Drang's relation to the Enlightenment was also closely bound up with another area of long-lasting critical dispute: the question of whether this youthful movement should be regarded as a fundamentally German phenomenon. Here too there has been a marked shift of opinion. While most critics in the inter-war years had no doubt that the Sturm und Drang grew out of the specific social and cultural conditions of the German states and was informed by a deep sense of national self-awareness, the thrust of most recent studies has been to emphasize the European context of the movement and in particular to stress the shaping influence of thinkers like Montesquieu, Diderot and Rousseau upon its development.[4]

Although there have undoubtedly been considerable advances in the study of the Sturm und Drang in the past decade or so, it is clear that there are still many areas of unresolved critical disagreement. The works of scholars like Hinck, Glaser, Dann, Schulte-Sasse and Huyssen have been particularly successful in extending our understanding of the historical situation in which the Sturm und Drang came into being and in laying bare the political-social and ideological presuppositions which governed its development.[5] They have been far less successful on the whole in assimilating these findings to a more penetrating and sensitive literary-critical analysis of the main works of the movement. The rigorous, discriminated research of the past years has certainly laid the basis for renewed attempts at such an analysis and provided indeed a very powerful incentive for them.

The following study concentrates on the drama which the writers of the Sturm und Drang (like Lessing) saw as the most sophisticated and powerful literary form of their time — the form in which they could express themselves most strongly, fully and directly, and through which they could have an effective and immediate impact upon the contemporary world. One of my main concerns will be to examine how this group of questing writers, bound together by the force of their shared experience of estrangement and dissent, attempted to use the drama as the vehicle of their impelling and quite distinctive experience of crisis.

To do justice to these diverse, complex works we have constantly to probe the ways in which the various playwrights attempted to reach out towards new dramatic structures in order to confront the kinds of experience they felt to be urgently and inalienably their own. This drive to iconoclasm and experiment forms a vital part of their artistic self-awareness as a group. They were all in their different ways committed to the belief doctrinally stated by Gerstenberg in his *Merkwürdigkeiten*:

⫣ Wo Genie ist, da ist Erfüllung, da ist Neuheit, da ist das Original.[6]

But we can't stop here. To evaluate the quest of the young dramatists for innovation and renewal, we have also to ask to what extent it was founded on, and perhaps constrained by, notions of what the drama was and could achieve as a literary form, of its power to focus and communicate experience and to affect the minds of those who responded to it. We have, in other words, to try also to guage the pressure of traditional assumptions at work in the overt, flambuoyant will of the Stürmer und Dränger to challenge tradition.

Underlying this study is the conviction that only a pains-taking attempt to sound these and other tensions informing the conception of the individual plays of the 1770's can help us gain a fuller grasp of the various, often contradictory, imaginative impluses which make the Sturm und Drang such an ambiguous, provocative — and still deeply involving — movement.

Chapter 1

THE DRAMATIC THEORY OF THE STURM UND DRANG: HERDER, LENZ, MERCIER

I

The discussion of the drama in the Sturm und Drang took place in the shadow of the *Hamburgische Dramaturgie*. All the young writers who were concerned with the reform and the renewal of the drama shared Lessing's belief in its power to help bring about far-reaching changes in the social and cultural life of the nation as a whole, and they were all convinced in one way or another of the vital historical importance of Lessing's radical critical engagement with the drama. His penetrating enquiry into the nature of the dramatic form, his will to advocate a new kind of 'bürgerlich' drama relevant to the needs of contemporary society and above all his rigorous questioning of some of the most widely-held assumptions of classicist dramaturgy – all of this acted both as a stimulus and a provocation on the disaffected, aspiring young writers of the 1770's. The impact of the *Hamburgische Dramaturgie* went far beyond this, however. Looking back we can see how clearly Lessing marked out the central areas of critical enquiry which were to pre-occupy the younger generation. Lessing was the first critic to confront the problem of the dramatic tradition openly and in a spirit of radical questioning.[1] He it was who posed the fundamental question of how the two main developments of the modern drama – in Elizabethan England and in 17th-century France – were related to that of classical Greece. Moreover, he had pursued these enquiries not in a spirit of detached academic enquiry but with an immediate burning concern to explore the ways in which the drama might develop in late 18th-century Germany.

The *Hamburgische Dramaturgie* thus provided a clear, challenging and unavoidable framework for ongoing critical discussion. It opened up the vast issues which the following generation had to confront and provided a cohesive body of critical assumptions, judgements and aims against which the young reformers could measure and clarify their passionately held, but to a large extent undefined, ambitions. Like Lessing they felt impelled to question the situation of the drama in the present by means of a sustained

15

critical engagement with the central dramatic tradition — and above all with the work of Shakespeare. A fuller, revitalised understanding of the work of the Elizabethan playwright, they assumed, was crucial to a new awareness of how the drama could regain its supreme imaginative authority in the contemporary world.[2]

In the following discussion I would like to concentrate attention mainly on the three most substantial and innovative statements of dramatic theory in the early 1770's. In two of these, Herder's justly famous *Shakespeare* essay and Lenz's *Anmerkungen übers Theater*, the English playwright is at the very centre of critical preoccupation, while in the third, Louis-Sébastien Mercier's *Du Théâtre. Nouvel Essai sur l'art dramatique*, which had a great impact in Germany, the writer (although also interested in Shakespeare) is concerned primarily to clarify his own aims and practice as a socially engaged, progressive dramatist. These seminal statements of dramatic theory all had a long and complex genesis and overlap chronologically. Herder wrote the first version of his essay on Shakespeare in 1771 and revised it in the following year before publishing a third and final version in *Von deutscher Art und Kunst* in 1773.[3] Lenz delivered a large part of what was to become his *Anmerkungen übers Theater* as a lecture in Straßburg in 1771. He extensively rewrote and developed this in the course of the following two years, however, and only succeeded with Goethe's help in finally publishing the essay as we know it in 1774.[4] Mercier's *Nouvel Essai* for its part did not appear until 1773. However, he had already explored many of the ideas developed here in shorter, fragmentary form in the forewords to his individual plays throughout the four previous years.[5]

When Herder set out to develop his new and revolutionary thoughts on Shakespearean drama he was aware of taking part in a developing critical discussion. Both his friend Gerstenberg and Lessing had recently expressed controversial and largely opposing views of the conception and character of Shakespeare's work and these views clearly acted as a stimulus to Herder's own thinking.[6]

In the *Hamburgische Dramaturgie* Lessing had attempted to show that Shakespeare was the true heir to the Greek classical dramatists because his plays had the same supreme power to evoke the tragic emotions of pity and fear. He, not Corneille, fulfils the laws of tragedy laid down once and for all by Aristotle.[7] The crucial presupposition of Lessing's argument here is that the essential

16

imaginative character of a drama is shaped not by its external form or modes of presentation, but by its power to grip and affect the responding mind. This concern to penetrate beyond the structural characteristics of a play to the inner force of its imaginative impact enables him to put Shakespeare forward as the supreme modern dramatist, and at the same time to discredit neo-classical French tragedy as a derivative, imaginatively sterile mode. The thrust of Lessing's argument is to play down the historical gulf separating the drama of ancient Greece from that of Shakespeare and to present them both as modes which in different ways fulfil the laws of the tragic form which had been defined once and for all by Artistotle.

In this respect Gerstenberg's approach to the Elizabethan dramatist is more radical and iconoclastic. In his discussion in the 14th part of his *Literaturbriefe* (which was written in 1766) he sets out to detach the plays of Shakespeare from the traditions of classical tragedy and to present them as modern works shaped by a quite different sense of artistic purpose.[8] Unlike the Greek tragedians Shakespeare — Gerstenberg insists — does not aim primarily to excite pity and fear but rather to bring to life a whole, particularised world, to realise powerful individual characters. He concedes that Shakespeare's plays may well have a cathartic effect but claims that this is subsidiary to his main concern to recreate the actuality of life (56 ff.). In Gerstenberg's view we should not approach Shakespearean drama as tragedy in any traditional sense but as a more general kind of play which he describes as 'lebendige Bilder der sittlichen Natur' (59). In the 15th letter Gerstenberg elaborates this view of the essentially realistic impetus of Shakespeare's imagination by comparing *Othello* with Edward Young's play *The Revenge*. Whereas Young, in attempting to arouse pity and horror in the mind of the spectator, is content to realise an abstract awareness of the disruptive tragic force of jealousy, Shakespeare seeks to grasp the specific workings of this obsessive passion in the mind of a unique individual in a particular situation. He observes the motives of the characters, in other words, with close and scrupulous attention (61 ff.). *Othello*, like *Macbeth* and *Hamlet*, he concludes, are essentially character-plays — not enactments of a tragic plot but the fully realised portrayal of individual human beings (57 ff.).

Herder was clearly influenced by this new and challenging approach to Shakespearean drama and wrote his own essay in its original form for publication in Gerstenberg's *Schleswigische Literaturbriefe*. Like his friend, Herder proceeds from a primary awareness of Shakespearean drama as something formally separate from, and alien to, Greek classical tragedy. He is, however, also concerned, as Lessing had been, to assert its essentially tragic character. His attempts to pursue the twofold aim, however, take him far beyond the assumptions and methods of both Gerstenberg and the *Hamburgische Dramaturgie*.

II

In his essay Herder attempts to open up a new and transforming understanding of Shakespearean drama as the complete organic expression of the historical world in which it came into being. In contrast to Goethe's brief lyrical testimony to the genius of Shakespeare, in which he expresses his inspiring sense of kinship, of intense spiritual closeness to the great English dramatist, Herder is aware that he is emphasizing the historical gulf between himself and Shakespeare and between the drama of Elizabethan England and the kinds of play which could embrace the particular historical-social conditions of Europe in the late 18th century.[9] Nonetheless, despite his concern to locate and thus relativize historically the work of Shakespeare, his reflections are charged with the belief that a radically new, more penetrating understanding of the Elizabethan playwright is crucial to the regeneration of German literature in the present: that a fuller grasp of the rootedness of his drama in the conditions of 16th-century England can drive the aspiring young writers in the 1770's to a more searching confrontation with themselves and the world in which they live.

Throughout his essay Herder is intent on emphasizing the fundamental paradox of Shakespeare's creative power. He presents the dramatist as the product of a complex transitional period in the growth of the modern world, as a man of his time who is conditioned intellectually, emotionally and spiritually by the pressures of life in Elizabethan England. At the same time, however, he also extols Shakespeare as the supreme genius who creates reality out of

18

his own limitless, unsearchable energies. Herder does not shrink, in fact, from likening the playwright to the divine Creator, for Shakespeare too – he insists – brings into being entire worlds which (like the natural creation) are informed throughout by the will of their creator (227). In Herder's view the creativity of Shakespeare is sovereign. It is subject to no conventions or laws except those given in his own poetic will. He creates in full spontaneous freedom out of himself, and yet, Herder claims, his work penetrates and reveals the whole existing world. In pursuing the impulses of his own imaginative vision he grasps the driving energies of life itself (221 f.). For Herder this paradox of Shakespeare's creativity is inherent in the fundamentally religious impetus of his imagination. He does not see the dramatist's creative mind as merely responding to, or impelled by, the awareness of the divine in the world around him (for this would imply an essential separation or detachment), but rather existing in a fathomless, mystical harmony with the creative power of God as this realises itself in the movements of nature and history – as the organ and manifestation of this power. Shakespeare's work is thus for Herder in a real sense revelation. The conception of his plays is pragmatic and transcendental, empirical and visionary at one and the same time: they are the ultimate imaginative realisation of his age in the perspective of eternity.

In the first part of his essay Herder tries to grasp the individuality of the Shakespearean dramatic mode by contrasting it with the plays of ancient Greece. This complex, richly discriminated form has in fact little more than the name in common with Greek drama (210). The structural unity of classical drama reflects, as Herder sees it, the simplicity and coherence of the Greek view of life. This was an inherently unified outlook which embraced religious, political and moral attitudes in an organic, harmonious whole – a wholeness which the dramatist could articulate in a clear, integrated dramatic action (210 ff.). Shakespeare, by contrast, confronted a world teemingly various and disjointed, a world torn by harsh, colliding tensions and haunted by the threat of disruption and chaos (217 ff.). Ambitions, loyalties and fears seem here to collide and overlap in ways which no individual could oversee, much less control. So many designs run together, so many conflicts intersect that, it would seem, no dramatist could encompass them all in a binding, cohesive structure. And yet this is precisely what in Herder's view Shakespeare achieves:

19

Er fand ... ein Vielfaches von Ständen, Lebensarten, Gesinnungen, Völkern und Spracharten ...; er dichtete also Stände und Menschen, Völker und Spracharten, König und Narren, Narren und König zu dem herrlichen Ganzen (218).

Herder is here passionately refuting the conventional assumption that this wide-ranging, diverse, realistic form of Shakespeare's is fragmented and shapeless. It *has* a structure, but this is not, he insists, the fixed, preconceived structure of French classical drama which is, as it were, imposed from without on the content of the play (213 ff.). The form of Shakespearean drama is organic, living, implicit in the driving tensions which the dramatist divines in the world around him. In Herder's view the complex movements of the action in the plays of Shakespeare are the direct manifestation or embodiment of the processes determining the life of contemporary society. His plays are in a quite literal sense 'dramatic history' 221), just as history in its tense, remorseless progressions is intrinsically dramatic in character. This inward, organising impetus of the Shakespearean form Herder terms 'Begebenheit', in order to separate it from what he sees as the fixed, mechanistic concept of action ('Handlung') in French drama.[10] Action in the Shakespearean sense is not a unilinear development of plot, but an inherent, animating force which holds together and informs all the diverse characters and events which make up the discordant world of the play.

This is the soul of the play, its life-giving core. Yet despite its shaping and sustaining force it is not something which lends itself to detached analytical intelligence — which can be isolated and dissected as a separate entity. It is accessible only to the intuitive imagination of the reader or spectator, when this is wholly possessed by the dramatic spectacle. Only the individual who inhabits the world of the play and is completely taken over by it can perceive the emergent order in this perplexing welter of seemingly contingent actions and events, and in so doing respond inwardly to the controlling movement of the dramatist's shaping will:

Wie vor einem Meere von Begebenheit, wo Wogen in Wogen rauschen, so tritt vor seine Bühne! Die Auftritte der Natur rücken vor und ab; wirken ineinander, so disparat sie scheinen; bringen sich hervor und zerstören sich, damit die Absicht des Schöpfers, der alle im Plane der Trunkenheit und Unordnung gesellet zu haben schien, erfüllt werde ... (220)

Herder is clearly out to set this new and challenging view of the organic, living form of Shakespearean drama against conventional notions of the dramatic and, as we have seen, so discredit what he regards as the fixed, deadening norms of classicist dramaturgy. But he is also using it, though less obviously, to override the rigid distinction between political and domestic drama which the theorists of the *bürgerliche Drama* from Diderot to Lessing had emphasized in order in effect to remove the drama out of the sphere of public events into the confined and ordered world of familial relations. Herder insists that Shakespeare's vision of the determining agency of history at work in every area of man's existence sweeps aside all such arbitrary divisions of genre. He is intent on showing that in Shakespearean drama conflicts between parent and child, brother and brother are shaped (like the struggles for political power) by the attempts of the individual to confront the pressures of his political-social situation (220 ff.). He shows, for example, that though the tragedy of Lear the King arises out of a familial crisis, this crisis is itself part of that great political-social process which shapes the life of the nation as a whole and inescapably controls its destiny. The family feud is rooted in corporate disorder and serves to bring this disorder to the point of irreversible crisis. The same is true, Herder states with sweeping assurance, of plays as different as the Histories and *Romeo and Juliet*. In all of these the passions and conflicts which form the main dramatic action arise out of a situation of collective upheaval and have the effect of further heightening these rending tensions in the life of society (220 ff.).

In these brief, far-reaching comments Herder is making a fundamental twofold assertion. In the world of Shakespearean drama, he insists, every experience, every event, is grounded in and manifests the determining impetus of history. But the converse is equally true. It is only in the sufferings and actions of individual human beings that these vast engulfing movements of history become flesh and find their consummation. Every man, be he king, chamberlain, beggar or fool, is for Shakespeare (Herder declares) at once the victtim and protagonist of history – his life is impelled by its relentless power and he is the indispensable agent of its unfolding.

This is for Herder the heart of Shakespeare's artistic achievement. The dramatist does not just evoke the totality of his age in all its discordant diversity; he *realises* it as a dynamic living force animated by the unsearchable will of God. He illuminates the world of

21

his time, makes it transparent to ultimate religious meaning and thus enables the spectator to affirm it as the vehicle of divine power. In responding to Shakespeare's plays the spectator in Herder's view is gripped more and more by the mystery of God's impenetrable will and is able in the end to affirm the world in awesome reverence and trust.

Implicit in Herder's view of Shakespearean tragedy is the awareness of a gulf between the developing and finally reconciling understanding of the spectator and the necessarily restricted outlook of the dramatic figures. The spectator who is able to participate more and more profoundly in the transforming vision of the dramatist, attains in Herder's view to a freeing metaphysical assurance which is denied the characters on stage who remain till the end the victims of an overwhelming, impenetrable world. However deeply the spectator identifies himself imaginatively with the tragic agents, he is always in some degree distanced from them by the force of his fuller encompassing awareness. Herder does not pursue the implications of this ironic clash of perspectives but his whole approach to Shakespeare's tragedies is informed by a tendency to qualify the significance of the passions and designs of the individual characters – to see through them, as it were, to the impelling momentum of history which is the final and necessary ground of the whole tragic enactment. Although he does at times extol the power of Shakespeare to bring to life strikingly individualised and impressive figures and to realise their destinies with intense involving force, it is always in the end the wider cosmic drive of the dramatist's imagination which grips his attention and governs his concern. Shakespeare is for him above all the 'große Schöpfer von Geschichte und Weltseele' (231) who illuminates to the responding mind a universe none of the protagonists can fully apprehend.

Herder makes his powerful plea for a new liberating unterstanding of the work of Shakespeare in the belief that this could stimulate far-reaching changes in contemporary German drama. He acknowledges, however, that he stops his discussion at the point where a genuine dramatic critic might well begin it (229 ff.)[11] He concedes that he does not discuss the crucial problem of how the playwright transforms a conventional story or romance into an integrated, dynamic organism, that he does not offer, in fact, an analysis of the formal structure of Shakespearean tragedy. This, however, is a larger and more basic omission than Herder himself

22

seems to realize, for this question he refuses to explore involves not just problems of dramatic method and practice but the more fundamental one of how Shakespeare sees and evaluates the agency of his characters, how he apprehends the interaction of subjective will and opposing circumstance in the unfolding development of the dramatic action.

Herder deliberately refrains from engaging such basic and at the same time practical considerations even though he must have realized that they are very relevant to the discussion of the ways in which the drama in Germany could develop in the late 18th-century. His role, as he evidently sees it, is to provide a radical perspective, a way of approaching and appreciating the unique genius of Shakespeare which will enable those young writers who seek fundamental literary reforms to confront these and other similarly vital issues in a spirit of independent and radical enquiry.

III

Lenz's reflections on the drama in *Anmerkungen übers Theater* are fired, like those of Herder, by a decisive encounter with the work of Shakespeare. Unlike Herder, however, Lenz does not set out to explore the historical rootedness of Shakespeare's work, its dependence on the particular social-cultural conditions of 16th-century England. His aim is more straightforward and more directly polemical. He presents Shakespeare as the creator of a specifically modern kind of character-drama which is Christian in inspiration and still enjoys the same supreme artistic authority in the late 18th-century as it did at the time of its conception. In order to elucidate the character and significance of Shakespearean drama – and this means for him above all Shakespearean tragedy – Lenz counterposes it repeatedly throughout his essay with neo-classical French drama which he sees as the derivative and lifeless issue of an artificial and outworn culture. His polemic strategy is to confront these different kinds of drama, to present them as morally and aesthetically antithetical. He extols Shakespeare in a way which serves to discredit the French classical drama, and dissects the latter as a means of emphasizing the supreme imaginative power and significance of the Elizabethan playwright.

23

French classical drama, as Lenz interprets it, has its roots in the theatre of ancient Greece and is shaped, like its antique forebear, by the fatalism of Greek religion, which proclaimed man's helplessness before the forces determining his existence.[12] The organising principle of Greek or Aristotelian drama is in Lenz's view the plot — the concatenation of external developments. He points out that the playwrights of ancient Greece were not interested in the individual as a moral agent, but only in the events which befell him, in his vulnerability to disaster. To the Greeks the plot was all-important for it embodied and symbolised the inexorable working of fate. Thus when Artistotle defines the drama in terms of an unfolding action he is acknowledging quite rightly (Lenz contends) the fundamentally religious character of the drama of his time (358). It is, however, absurd, indeed blasphemous, that modern French playwrights should take over a form conditioned by a superstitious, heathen religiosity and continue to use it in a way which denies the uniqueness and sanctity of the individual, his freedom to choose and act, which are for Lenz the primal assertions of Christianity.

The antithesis of this rigid, plot-controlled classical drama is, as Lenz sees it, the nordic, Shakespearean form which arises out of the primary energy of the free individual (343). Goethe, like Gerstenberg before him, had already emphasized Shakespeare's supreme power as a creator of characters, but Lenz goes much further than either. He defines Shakespearean drama as a form wholly devoted to the protrayal of the heroic protagonist. It celebrates his freedom and power in his confrontation with the world around him:

> Es ist die Rede von Charakteren, die sich ihre Begebenheiten erschaffen, die selbständig und unveränderlich die ganz große Maschine selbst drehen ...; nicht von Bildern, von Marionettenpuppen — von Menschen (343; cf. 345; 359).

The hero in Shakespearean drama, as Lenz sees it, initiates and controls the action and through it realizes his unique creative individuality. Lenz, in fact, goes so far as to claim that the different events which make up the dramatic development in Shakespeare's plays gain coherence and meaning solely from the fact that they show forth the supreme selfhood of the hero; this is not just their source but also their artistic *raison d'être*. The dramatist, as Lenz sees it, is faced by a clear choice between two fundamentally

24

opposed kinds of drama. He must either commit himself to a form determined by the individual, or to a form which subordinates character to the arbitrary motions of plot. Underlying Lenz's argument is the conviction that the existence of the free individual has a final metaphysical significance which separates it from ordinary contingent phenomena (343 ff.). It thus has in his view a reality which is clear and unassailable, and in a genuine sense independent of the playwright: it is not susceptible to the arbitrary workings of his subjective imagination. It is only when the dramatist is face to face with the reality of the free unconditioned self that he can (as Lenz sees it) be sure that he transcends the compulsions and fantasies which confuse his attempts to grasp the ordinary world of circumstance around him (351 f.). Those 'Aristotelian' dramatists who devote themselves to the manipulative intricacies of plot have in fact, Lenz argues, recoiled from the supreme reality of life into the treacherous sphere of their own imagination. Their plays are random acts of self-indulgence, 'willkürliche Tänze', which betray the compulsions of their own subjectivity but have no relation to the actual world they claim to represent (352). The Shakespearean drama, by contrast, is for Lenz realistic in the fullest possible sense. Its power to possess the responding imagination reveals the unique power of the playwright to open himself to the contemplation of free, impassioned humanity which he is able to recreate with vivid imaginative intensity. This is a particularising, psychological mode which realises a 'Mannigfaltigkeit der Charaktere und Psychologien' (351; cf. 341) and penetrates to the deepest springs of motive and feeling.

The driving exuberance of Lenz's commitment to Shakespearean drama and his belief in its directing authority tend to hide a deep, unresolved tension in his view which he himself clearly does not recognize. He sees the plays of Shakespeare as determined by two fundamental impulses which are essentially different in kind and to some extent inevitably in conflict. Throughout most of his essay he presents the English dramatist as the supreme advocate of personal freedom who celebrates the power of the heroic individual to transcend and dominate his environment. In some parts of his discussion, however, he is intent on stressing Shakespeare's powers as a psychological realist who penetrates to the deepest forces determining the individual's existence. Here he puts the dramatist forward as the remorseless analyst of the human psyche. This probing realistic drive, which he attributes to Shakespeare's creative imagination, his will to grasp the motives of his characters in an unfolding psychological process, presupposes a rigorous empirical mode of apprehension on the part of the playwright which is at odds with the basic trend of Lenz's interpretation. As a psychological realist he sees Shakespeare as exposing the inner causality governing the individual's actions — a causality which reveals the limitations of a particular character as he struggles to control the specific circumstances of his environment. Such an apprehension of the dramatic agents and the means of presentation it involves are inescapably in conflict with that visionary awareness of personal autonomy and power which Lenz sees as the deepest animating core of Shakespeare's inspiration.

Lenz, however, does not question how these different impulses are bound up and interact in the conception of Shakespeare's plays. He simply takes it for granted that they somehow mutually support one another. In the end in any case he tends largely to ignore the realistic, psychological dimension in the playwright's vision in order to assert the more strongly his view of Shakespeare as the advocate of free heroic individuality.

This exposes what is perhaps the main critical limitation of Lenz's polemic. He is so intent on portraying Shakespeare as the proponent of a radical modern individualism that he is forced to sweep aside or minimise any consideration which qualifies this view. This one-sidedness is most evident in his failure to get to grips with Shakespearean drama as the enactment of a tragic conflict, even though this is nominally at the centre of his concern. Indeed, his unqualified affirmation of the heroic protagonist seems to preclude any notion of tragic contradiction, however we define it. Lenz discusses the dramatic action solely in terms of the self-realization of the hero, and the presuppositions of the tragic conflict — the hero's collision with the world around him and his deepening experience of division and subjection — these all lie beyond his concern. Lenz consistently sees the hero as a source of unbroken, organic power in conflict with a world which thwarts his inborn potentialities. His reading of Shakespearean drama is informed by an awareness of a primal contradiction between the inner life of the self and the conditions of its existence in the corporate world. Shakespearean tragedy, as he sees it, expresses the revolt of the socially imprisoned and estranged individual who seeks to realize the God-given, passionate energies within him.

26

It is noticeable, however, that Lenz does not state this view openly, much less explore its implications for a new understanding of tragedy in the contemporary world. His reticence in this respect is in marked contrast to the directness of his polemic in other parts of his essay and probably betrays an uneasy feeling that this argument was driving him towards a quite new kind of tragic awareness for which he could no longer claim the full authority of Shakespeare. His encounter with the Elizabethan dramatist seems in fact to have forced him into a twofold impasse. On the one hand, it led him to envisage a tragedy of social estrangement which he sensed was not compatible with the categories of Shakespearean tragedy and which he therefore was reluctant to assert. At the same time, he was forced to recognize that these categories were in themselves quite alien to the realities of life in 18th-century German society. This again was a recognition which he did not fully face in this essay, although his review of *Götz von Berlichingen* (written probably about the same time as his final revision of the *Anmerkungen*) shows that it was playing on his mind. Although in this review he is also out to assert the individual's powers of free, creative action, his reflections are haunted by an awareness of the exposure of modern man to the complex, interlocking determinants which make up his social environment (378 ff.). For all his overt moral assurance it is clear that his imagination is gripped by a vision of the individual trapped in the vast inscrutable processes of a world which controls his existence and shapes his inner responses.

In my view it is quite wrong to see Lenz (like, for example, Inbar)[13] as interpreting Shakespeare in a way which allows him to clarify and assert his own creative aims as an aspiring playwright. His confrontation with the English dramatist seems rather to have had a deeply disturbing, disorientating impact both on his view of the possibilities of the drama in the society of his time and of his own potentialities as a playwright. His troubled confrontation with Shakespearean tragedy seems to issue in a pervading experience of dislocation and loss with which he does not fully come to terms. It was in this experience, however, that there came into being a fuller and more challenging vision of the comedy as the ironic, bitterly questioning, parodistic form most fully responsive to the tensions of life in contemporary society.

IV

Unlike any German commentator in the 1770's Louis-Sébastien Mercier was concerned to provide a full and coherent critical examination of the drama. Although his reflections were related to a large extent to the history and situation of the drama in France, they had a great and frutiful impact in Germany.[14] The appeal of Mercier's theoretical writings obviously stemmed in some measure from his approach. He discusses the drama as a knowledgeable and successful playwright who has experienced the practical problems of the theatre at first hand, yet who for all his commonsense and caution, still believes that a reformed, revitalised drama can regain its rightful place at the heart of the cultural and moral life of society. His dramaturgical reflections represent in the first place an attempt to understand and justify his objectives as a socially engaged, practising playwright and to place them in a significant historical perspective. These reflections culminate in his vast, comprehensive treatise *Du Théâtre. Nouvel Essai sur l'art dramatique* which appeared in 1773 and was translated into German at Goethe's instigation by Wagner in 1776.

Mercier's main practical aim in the *Nouvel Essai* is to advocate by means of a full critical discussion a new form of realistic domestic play which he terms the *drame*. Here, as in some of his earlier writings, he tries to demonstrate the need for this new kind of drama by emphasizing the irrelevance of tragedy to the conditions of modern life. Tragedy, as Mercier interprets it, is a political mode which can only thrive in a society in which the individual embraces both the private and the public worlds as the one indivisible arena of his moral existence.[15] Tragedy, in other words, presupposes the capacity to experience life as an organic whole, and this is only possible when the individual is aware of participating, responsibly and effectively, in the running of the state. In its fullest sense tragedy only existed (Mercier claims) in ancient Greece, where it grew out of the republican constitution of Athens and expressed the assertive civic pride which held together actor, playwright and spectator in a shared moral confidence (9 f.). The individual in the absolutist state lacks all such assurance, for his feeling of control in his private life is at odds with his sense of impotence as a political subject. His consciousness of himself is thus irrevocably divided. Mercier insists that if the drama is to regain its moral authority it

28

must address itself to this fissure at the very heart of the individual's experience in the contemporary world. Only a new kind of drama rooted in the actual world of the spectator can grip and transform his imaginative awareness and help him see himself and his world with new eyes. The *drame*, as Mercier defines it, is a realistic form which gives a powerful image of familial existence not as something separate and complete in itself but – and this is crucial – as part of the total, ongoing process of corporate existence (140 ff.). In so doing, it can rekindle his consciousness of involvement in society and stimulate his belief in his power to contribute to it in a significant, responsible way.

Mercier's sense of the moralising, didactic possibilities of the *drame* is closely bound up with his conviction that its flexible, realistic character is particularly appropriate to the complex, increasingly empirical character of contemporary experience. Once again he tries to press his argument by showing the irrelevance of tragedy to modern life. Tragedy, he insists, is not just impossible on social-political grounds but also on aesthetic ones (94 ff.). The way people experience reality in the everyday world is completely incompatible with the kind of formal organisation and intense stylisation which are the presupposition of the tragic mode. They are aware of reality as disparate and fluid, and feel themselves besieged by conflicting impressions which cannot be reduced to a clear, unified formula (104 ff.). The playwright who seeks to realise a strong, involving illusion of reality must mirror the tensions and incongruities of lived experience, and grasp the full diversity of emotions and moods which make up the continuum of real life – a diversity which traditional genres, both tragic and comic, have sacrificed to their search for an artificial purity of form (110 ff.). In this respect too the *drame* with its open, inclusive form – Mercier insists – is the most appropriate medium of contemporary experience. It overrides the arbitrary, conventional separation of genres and embraces the modes of experience and presentation traditionally associated with both tragedy and comedy. It is able to combine the passion and pathos of tragedy with the close observation of personal and communal existence typical of comedy; it can hold together the august and the everyday in one coherent structure and integrate these conflicting elements in an all-embracing, unified vision which is true to the wholeness of life and thus morally and aesthetically satisfying (137; 143 ff.; 178; 247 f.; 295).

Mercier, we can see, is placing the *drame* in the forefront of the struggle for a sharper, more differentiated social realism. He is aware that modern playwrights have to go to new lengths to overcome the initial scepticism and detachment of the spectator and to draw him into acceptance of the world presented on the stage (140; 144 ff.; 177 f.; 256; 265). Nonetheless it is clear that Mercier does not regard realism as an end in itself. He sees the detailed, particularising methods of the *drame* as subserving its main didactic purpose of observing and illuminating life in society. If the new form is to become 'l'école des vertus et des devoirs du citoyen', it must instruct. Its first aim must be to open up society for the spectator, show him what it is really like. And this means that the playwright must greatly extend the range of his social observation; he must attempt to illuminate whole areas of corporate life which have been ignored by the theatre. Mercier is aware that the kind of domestic drama he is advocating here breaks with traditional kinds which tend to see the life of the family as a sphere of activity complete in itself. The aim of the *drame*, as he defines it, is precisely to relate the sphere of familial relationships to the wider world of society in a new and significant manner, and in so doing help overcome the individual's feeling of estrangement from the state.

This is most evident in the way in which Mercier develops his view of the instructional, moral function of the *drame*. This new 'genre utile' illuminates the social environment of the individual, helps him to see his personal existence as part of an enclosing, sustaining whole. Mercier attaches great importance to this probing, critical function of the new drama. He emphasizes the fact that the theatre is the only real forum of public discussion and that the dramatist must therefore assume the moral obligation of exposing those forces which create suffering and conflict in the contemporary world. He has a particular responsibility to those who suffer unheard and unaided. He is, Mercier declares in a much quoted passage, 'l'interprète des malheureux, l'orateur public des opprimés' (135).

This is certainly the most innovative and radical aspect of Mercier's discussion in the *Nouvel Essai*. It is perhaps not surprising that it has attracted great attention and that critics have sometimes assumed that it represents the central concern of his whole treatise.[16] We have to realise, however, that Mercier sees the socially critical role of the *drame* in the context of its ultimate reconciliatory purpose. This new form, as he sees it, denounces the evils in society in order finally to demonstrate the power of human beings to control their social environment (pp. 233 ff.). The whole impetus of Mercier's discussion here leaves no doubt that he sees social protest as offset, and in the end transcended by, the revelation of the inner strength of those who suffer and of the capacity for renewal of those who have enslaved and demeaned their fellowmen. The *drame*, as Mercier defines it, is an essentially integrative, reconciliatory mode. It holds together seemingly incongruous points of view and kinds of perception and creates a continuity between the different contexts in which the individual lives out his life. It aims to realize a diverse but finally harmonious sense of the totality of existence. The primary aesthetic and didactic function of the new form, as Mercier conceives it, is to unify an immediate, detailed observation of social relationships with an affirmative moral view of the inner strength of the dramatic agents. It presents conflicts which are rooted in the tensions of contemporary society but shows that these conflicts can be resolved by individuals who have the power to transcend the attitudes and aims imposed on them by their class position and outlook – individuals who are able to see through and redirect their lives in accordance with the deeper imperatives within them.

It is evident throughout Mercier's discussion that he sees a considerable tension between empirical insight and moral awareness as fundamental to the conception of the *drame*. He does not seem conscious, however, of how sharp and disruptive the opposition between these two impulses really is, or of how difficult it would be in practice to realize the kind of imaginative synthesis which be outlines in theoretical terms. Certainly he never enters into any detailed discussion of the immense problems facing the dramatist who attempts to bring analytical and moral insights into effective interaction or of the developments of form and technique which such a delicate and difficult undertaking would necessarily involve.

V

These three seminal statements of dramatic theory differ considerably, as I have tried to emphasize, in their methods and immediate aims. They all spring, it is true, from a common belief that the drama must undergo fundamental and far-reaching changes if it is to come to terms with the complexities of contemporary experience. Only Mercier, however, makes any attempt to describe and analyse these changes, and our examination shows in fact that all three writers (Mercier as much as his German counterparts) are in the last resort very uncertain about the character of the new realistic, socially responsive kinds of drama to which they aspire. These discussions all probe in new and varying ways the relationship between the drama as an aesthetic structure and the empirical world of historical-social reality. Whereas inherited classicist theories presupposed the essential autonomy of the drama as a personal, self-sufficient mode, these young critics see the dramatic world as bound up with, and dependent upon, the conditions of a particular social environment which crucially determines its character. None of them, however, comes to terms with the implications of this very significant change in the conception of the dramatic form. None of them really addresses the crucial problem of how a drama which is to a new degree empirical and analytic can embrace character and environment, personal agency and impersonal process in a coherent, developing structure. Herder, Lenz and Mercier all see the drama in keeping with received assumptions as embodying powerful and significant processes of interpersonal conflict but seem unsure about the ways in which new 'open', socially transparent forms can integrate these processes with the impetus of those historical-social forces which determine the wider situation of the dramatic figures. Herder for his part does seem aware of the vital importance of such questions but expressly refuses to investigate the ways in which Shakespeare dramatises the simple narratives which are his raw material, transforms them artistically into supremely powerful, significant historical tragedy. In the case of Lenz the situation is even more complex. He defines Shakespearean tragedy in a way which, as we have seen, presupposes the social estrangement of the hero yet which prevents him from acknowledging this as the basis of the tragic development. For although he is aware of the involvement of Shakespeare's hero in an alien, thwarting environment, Lenz nonetheless interprets what is in fact an expression of revolt as a manifestation of the unconditioned freedom of the creative individual. This view of the absolute autonomy of the hero necessarily precludes that shaping tension between self and world which Herder

32

sensed at the heart of Shakespearean tragedy and which also seems implicit in Lenz's own deepest intuitive responses.

It is, however, in Mercier's full and painstaking attempts to define the new form of domestic drama that this uncertainty is most obvious. Mercier, as we have seen, defines the *drame*, on the one hand, as a rigorous, realistic form which demonstrates the exposure of the characters to the pressures of their environment. At the same time, he makes it clear that this new mode must vindicate the moral freedom of the individual and show his power to transcend the constraints of a seemingly destructive social situation. Mercier, however, does not explore how the playwright can assimilate this deterministic view of human vulnerability to the finally triumphant vision of personal freedom and power. He evades any detailed discussion of the immense technical difficulties involved in the attempt to embrace the pressure of social-psychological determinants and responsible personal activity in a unified process of dramatic development. Inherent in his view of the new form there is a profound tension between conflicting methods and imaginative perspectives which he fails fully to acknowledge, much less seek to resolve.

This tension in Mercier's view of the *drame* shows in a specific and very blatant form a hesitancy which is apparent in these three dramaturgical enquiries. All are intent on advocating forms of drama which are realistic, able to express a penetrating view of the motivation of individualised characters. Such psychological realism necessarily entails a differentiated awareness of the involvement of the dramatic figures in the conditions of a particular social-historical situation which transcends the sphere of close interpersonal relationships at the centre of dramatic interest. It is also apparent, however, that all three critics in their different ways uphold the traditional view of the drama as an essentially metaphysical form. The drama, as they see it, illuminates human existence, makes it transparent to ultimate orders of significance. This brings us close to the heart of these dramaturgical reflections. Consciously or unconsciously these writers attribute to the drama a supreme power to bring together and harmonise a probing, analytical view of life and a cosmic vision of man's destiny. None of them, however, really confronts the crucial question of how a modern realistic play – and in particular a modern realistic tragedy – can come to terms with the relativising awareness of the individual's dependence on the pressures of his specific environment without undermining the drama's traditional preoccupation with the ultimate problems of his existence, or of how such metaphysical concerns can find new and vital roots in a close empirical scrutiny of his day-to-day life in society. This is a problem which we will have to consider again in some detail.

Chapter 2

GOETHE'S GÖTZ VON BERLICHINGEN.
INDIVIDUALITY AND HISTORY

Critics have always found it very hard to say in what precise
sense *Götz* is a historical play, that is to determine the ways in
which the historical awareness of the playwright informs and shapes
the imaginative conception of the drama. When in 1952 Sengle
pointed out that this is the first play in German literature which
sought to bring to life a total historical-social situation, he was
challenging accepted views of the work by emphasizing an aspect of
its conception which had been very largely neglected.[1] For many
years critics had concentrated their attention on the figure of the
hero in a way which relegated the play's historical dimension and
had the effect of dividing the drama in two. The attempts of scholars like von Wiese, Staiger and Kayser to see Götz as the embodiment of Goethe's vision of full organic individuality, of a 'Natur-
form des menschlichen Daseins', involved a marked tendency to
isolate the figure of the hero from its historical context.[2] Their
view of the protagonist presupposed an opposition between an
innate, metaphysically given self and the contingent forces of history. In their readings of the play the historical appears solely as a
blindly destructive force which negates the natural, human values
sublimely embodied in the character of the hero.

Discussions of *Götz* in the early sixties showed an increasing
dissatisfaction with this uncritically affirmative conception of the
protagonist. Ryder and Graham attempted in two re-directive interpretations to show that Götz was in fact a complex, problematic
figure driven by deeply contradictory impulses. From their different points of view both succeeded in developing a psychologically
discriminated view of the hero and his relations with those around
him.[3] All subsequent interpretations of the play owe much to these
two subtle and searching discussions, but they did nothing do
deepen our understanding of its historical character. In their preoccupation with the outlook and experience of the protagonist
both were quite clearly intent on regarding *Götz* as a character-
tragedy in which historical conditions have little relevance to the

central action. In the end, in fact, the interpretations of Graham and Ryder are as one-sided as those which they set out to reject. Fritz Martini was able to show this quite clearly in a very perceptive re-assessment of the drama in 1972.[4]

The main purpose of Martini's analysis was to establish the inner unity of *Götz* by revealing how character-play and historical-drama are inseparably bound up and mutually determine one another. But although he attempts to give a more diverse and balanced interpretation which integrates the different aspects of the play, it is clear that Martini too does not see the central tragic conflict as arising out of particular historical situation. He is concerned rather to show that the collision between Götz and his opponents is an essentially moral opposition — a conflict between good and evil the significance of which far transcends the specific historical tensions which the dramatist lays bare.[5] For Martini too there seems to be a gap between Goethe's far-reaching historical interest and the shaping impulses of his dramatic conception.

These different views of *Götz* reveal basic problems of interpretation which we must take seriously.[6] In their different ways they draw our attention to a fundamental area of difficulty and help to show us, I think, a valid starting-point for our attempts to re-examine the play. We must begin, it seems to me, by confronting the crucial question of how Goethe actually *sees* the relation between historical process and dramatic action in *Götz*. We must look again at the means by which the playwright explores the historical situation enclosing the dramatic development and seek to determine how far forces inherent in this situation affect the behaviour of the figures and their connections with one another.

Most critis, I think, would accept that the relation between Götz and Weislingen is central to Goethe's conception of the tragedy. The dramatist makes it quite clear that Weislingen is the driving, organising force behind the pursuit and final entrapment of the hero. At the same time Goethe emphasizes the intimate and highly personal character of the relationship between the two men who were close childhood friends. And it is this which has often disturbed critics. There seems to be — they have repeatedly claimed — a basic disparity between this relationship, so deeply conditioned by private, emotional pressures, and the wider historical-social tensions which the drama enacts. The opposition of these two men lacks (in this view) a wider representative dimension and this de-

36

tracts greatly from the historical significance of the work as a whole.

This is in fact a real difficulty. One cannot play down the deeply personal character of the relationship between the two adversaries. Götz experiences Weislingen's betrayal as a deeply demoralizing blow, and the dramatist shows that it marks the beginning of a process of inner attrition which ends in the hero's disabling experience of powerlessness and defeat. Götz has attached great importance to liberating Weislingen from the corrupting, enslaving influence of the court and to restoring to him the freedom and dignity of an imperial Knight (86 f.). When Weislingen breaks his promise and returns to the service of the Bishop of Bamberg Götz feels himself somehow exposed and diminished, and it is symptomatic that he refuses so long to believe that it has really happened (109 f.; 115 f.). It is noticeable that Götz is scarely aware of the political implications of Weislingen's betrayal. He is overcome rather by the pain of losing his former friend who was also to have become his brother-in-law. But the defection of Weislingen – as the dramatist makes clear – is of decisive political importance and forms in fact the turning-point in the fate of the hero. For it is Weislingen who co-ordinates the campaign of the princes against Götz. It is as if their thwarted, pent-up fury needed his single-minded and passionate hostility to give it direction and real destructive force. Weislingen it is who achieves the crucial step of moving the Emperor to take legal proceedings against Götz (122 f.). And once he has gained this authority Weislingen does not hesitate to manipulate the proceedings at Heilbronn in a way which, as he knows, must entrap Götz (146 f.). Even though his immediate aim is thwarted by the attack of Sickingen, Weislingen still enjoys a legal and military advantage which he is able to exploit to the full. He foresees clearly that once Götz has sworn 'Urfehde' he is lost: that sooner or later he must revolt against the inactivity which is quite unbearable to him and in so doing place himself once and for all outside the law (152). Thus when Götz allows himself to be persuaded into taking over command of the peasants' rebellion he is only doing – albeit in an extreme form – what Weislingen has all along anticipated. It is no surprise when Weislingen now appears at the head of the imperial forces, intent on seizing the opportunity finally to destroy Götz who is now openly identified with the enemies of the Emperor (164).

Goethe lays bare by probing analytical means the psychic compulsions underlying the implacable hostility of Weislingen. He shows that this is a man tortured by a deeplying sense of self-doubt and driven by a need he can scarely recognise to destroy the man who is in every way his superior (152). But Goethe's aim goes further. He seeks to relate these driving, irrational compulsions to the pressure bearing in upon the figure from his particular social environment: to show how he is uprooted and confused by the quickly changing economic-social conditions which control his experience in ways which he himself cannot understand. Seen from this point of view Goethe is in fact exploring Weislingen's behaviour as a means of grasping tensions in the historical situation which could not be revealed with such directness and subtlety by any other method.

Weislingen, as the dramatist presents him, is impelled by strong social, political and sexual aspirations which disorientate him and undermine his inner integrity. It is Adelheid von Walldorf who perceives the peculiar social insecurity of this man and who seeks to use it as a means of governing him completely. She rightly senses that he is dizzied by dreams of power and status released by the accelerating processes of social change. These dreams — she sees — drive him to realise himself both as a man and as a political agent in ways which he could not have envisaged even a few years before. In Weislingen, as Adelheid clearly perceives, erotic and social aspirations are indissolubly bound up and mutually intensify one another (111 f.). Her insight into his peculiar vulnerability is confirmed by Liebetraut:

Der Händedruck eines Fürsten, und das Lächeln einer schönen Frau! Da reißt sich kein Weislingen los (106).

Adelheid sets out to exploit the deep inner uncertainty of the opportunist who has cut himself off from his own class and now devotes himself wholly to the cause of the Princes. She recognises that the man who would be 'Herr von Fürsten' must find her, the beloved of princes, irresistible. It is this insight which gives her total power over him. Goethe is showing that in Weislingen's relentless desire to destroy Götz powerful, emotional and social impulses flow together with irresistible determining force. Malignant hostility towards the friend he has wronged is bound up with the conviction he has taken over from his masters that Götz is the real hindrance to their claims for greater political control and thus impedes the development of society towards stability and peace. The dramatist is further concerned to show that in taking over the assumptions and aims of the Princes Weislingen also adopts their political methods. The ruthless way he uses deceit, intrigue and treachery as the normal instruments of asserting power, the way he subjects all humane, moral considerations to narrow political ends – these are (the dramatist suggests) the distinctive means of the court. Indeed the unusual effectiveness of Weislingen in the diplomatic, political sphere stems from the skill with which he adopts these methods and exploits them single-mindedly to destroy his enemy. Goethe reveals how much Weislingen has conformed to the attitudes of the court by ironically counterposing his way of working with that of Adelheid. The brutal cunning with which Weislingen pursues and finally traps Götz is identical with that which she has used to ensnare Weislingen and subject him to her designs (105 f.; 111 f.; 122 f.).

This is not all, however. Goethe also seems at the same time to be pointing beyond the specific historical circumstances in which the action is set and to be attributing to the outlook and behaviour of Weislingen a more general political significance. The ruthless pursuit of power, the readiness to use all existing political and legal agencies as a means of lending this pursuit the appearance of propriety, the will to sacrifice all wider social concerns to the promotion of close, sectional interests – are these not still (Goethe seems to ask) the characteristic methods of the despotic German Princes? There can be little doubt that he expected his readers and spectators in the 1770's to judge Weislingen from their own direct experience of the German courts.

He seeks thus to realise the figure in a subtle and diverse way: to see him at one and the same time as the victim of historical forces he cannot understand and as the effective agent of an inexorable system of political control which is still operative in the contemporary world.

The dramatist, it seems to me, also expresses a similarly complex, differentiated view of the central figure, Götz. There can be no doubt that he is keen to celebrate the vital yet humane character of the 'Ritter mit der eisernen Hand', and affirms in it his longing (and that of his whole generation) for a dynamic, integrated and morally coherent way of life. No critic would deny this, but few have recognised the extent to which the dramatist sees Götz as a being engulfed by a historical crisis which he cannot oversee and which calls in question the very foundations of his spiritual existence.

The Princes, as we have seen, regard Götz as the source of serious social unrest and violence. In claiming for himself the traditional right to self-help he places himself knowingly, in their view, outside the existing order of society and challenges the authority of the Emperor. The spectator is obviously not meant to take this as a dispassionate view, since the Princes fear Götz primarily as the enemy of their own sectional interests. Götz himself in fact regards their remorseless opposition as the sure proof of the moral validity of his aims: as a testimony to his sincere selfless commitment to the good of the German nation and its people (90 f.). Goethe, however, does not allow us to identify ourselves fully with this view either, even though we are drawn to the Knight by the warmth, candour and magnaminity of his character. In the course of the action the playwright increasingly qualifies the self-understanding of the hero by a process of searching exposition which, although largely oblique, is nonetheless of fundamental importance for an understanding of the whole dramatic development. We can see this painstaking exploration of the historical world beyond the immediate sphere of the characters most clearly in two scenes which mark crucial stages in the campaign against Götz: that in which Adelheid succeeds in undermining Weislingen's sense of obligation to Götz and in drawing him back to the service of the Bishop of Bamberg (11, 6); and that in which Weislingen in turn overcomes the Emperor's deep unwillingness to take legal proceedings against Götz (111, 1). These scenes form decisive stages in the external development of the play, but they also fulfill an equally important expository function which we must observe closely.

In these two scenes the process of exposition takes place simultaneously on two levels. In the former Goethe presents Adelheid's behaviour as symptomatic of the basic tendencies of her social class. The skill with which she uses her beauty and manipulates the arguments in order to enslave Weislingen is characteristic of the depersonalised, domineering methods of the court. She makes no sincere attempt to find out the truth; she is concerned only to break Weislingen's resistance and gain complete power over him by any means whatever (112 f.). Goethe's concern to expose Adelheid and, through her, the Princes is clear and unmistakable. This encounter between Adelheid and Weislingen, however, is also the vehicle of another kind of exposition which is of just as great importance but which remains essentially inexplicit. What is revealed here is something negative — the inability of Weislingen to justify from any valid social or moral standpoint his commitment to Götz. Weislingen — it is clear — is struggling desperately to do this in order to assert his own moral credibility and dignity before the deriding Adelheid. Only a valid defence of his loyality to Götz could rehabilitate him in the eyes of this woman he wants so much to impress. It is noticeable, however, that he is completely unable to defend Götz's behaviour and the social ideals underlying it. He does, it is true, point to the great magnetic qualities of Götz's personality which have held him spell-bound but when Adelheid insists that as an ally of Götz Weislingen would become like him, 'ein Feind des Reichs ..., ein Feind der bürgerlichen Ruh und Glückseligkeit', he cannot reply (112 f.). Even beleaguered as he is Weislingen does not urge that in Götz's particular circumstances his claim to the right of self-help has a relative justification or that his moral aspirations are even partially defensible. No, at the end of the dispute Weislingen is forced to acknowledge what he has known all along: that in falling under Götz's influence he has allied himself with a man who threatens to thrust society into chaos.

Goethe is also concerned to underline this crucial distinction between Götz the moral individual and Götz the political agent in the encounter between Weislingen and the Emperor Maximilian in Act III. As in the scene just discussed, the dramatist forces us to look beneath the level of overt exposition. He reveals here once again the deviousness of Weislingen, who is now the committed representative of the Princes and who seeks to influence the Emperor and use his authority for his own ends. Goethe leaves no doubt that Weislingen is simulating an idealistic concern for the welfare of the Empire as a means of gaining an important political advantage — feigning loyalty to Maximilian as a means of bending the latter to his will. This is all made very clear. But in this scene too the exposition has a further, partially hidden, dimension. What is important once again — in obvious parallel to the former scene — is the failure of an individual who seeks to defend Götz to find any political or social justification for his behaviour. The Emperor is manifestly very reluctant to take action against Götz because he recognises the latter's loyalty and courage, and still hopes to be able to use these in the service of the Empire (122 f.). But he is quite unable to counter Weislingen's claim that one must not see Götz simply as one isolated, misguided individual but rather as the focus of all those forces of disorder and violence which threaten to disrupt the stability of the Empire. The activities of Götz — Weislingen points out — serve to release the 'Schwindelgeist, der ganze Landschaften ergreift', to mobilise forces over which he himself has no control. The Emperor in the end has to accept the conclusion that Götz does represent a serious threat to public order, to his own authority as the head of state. With gread sadness Maximilian agrees that legal proceedings should be instituted against him (123). The fact that the Emperor, who in his affection for Götz sees through the special pleading of Weislingen, should nonetheless be persuaded that Götz's activities undermine the order of society endorses the revelation of Götz's destabilising influence in the earlier scene. That Maximilian who stands outside all sectional interests and rivalries and is concerned only for the unity and long-term good of the Empire, should be forced to accept this negative view of Götz's political position is of great expository importance and must affect our understanding of the wider historical crisis.

These two scenes fulfill an important revelatory function.[7] We can only grasp this fully, however, if we see them in conjunction with the fourth scene of the first act which serves to illuminate the contemporary situation in a more discursive generalising way than any other scene in the play. Here Olearius, an idealistic academic lawyer, just returned from Rome, analyzes for his listeners the immense transitions in which the contemporary world is caught up. Society, he insists, is at a cross-roads in which there are possibilities of great cultural and social advance. The recent introduction of the system of Roman Law marks for Olearius one decisive means of re-integrating and renewing the Empire (94 f.). Society, he points out, had become too complex and sophisticated for the many, piece-meal, pragmatic systems of justice which had existed beforehand — systems which were too dependent on local circumstance and too easily distorted by ignorance and prejudice. The introduction of this new uniform and enlightened legal system will make possible more consistent and reliable judgements, and this in turn will help to bring about a more stable, harmonious society. In the course of this scene it becomes apparent that the Emperor shares

42

this belief of Olearius in the civilising, renewing possibilities of the new system of justice. His aim is to re-enforce the authority and standing of the institutions of law by sweeping aside archaic forms of feud and retribution and so to create a stable state of peace. The expository significance of this scene lies not only in the fact that it gives the spectator a wider view of the historical situation but rather that it clarifies the sense of far-reaching crisis, which all the characters share in one way or another, and places it in a different perspective. This period of transition in the view of the Emperor and of other men of good-will bears within it the possibility of significant constitutional and social progress. This volatile world in which new social groupings and power-constellations are coming into being precipitates the rise of opportunists like Weislingen and the quest of the Princes to increase their power, but it is also – as the Emperor sees it – a world in which great positive developments can take place and his directing aim is to create the political and legal institutions which can foster these developments.

The process of exposition begun in this significant scene near the beginning of the play and extended in the two scenes previously discussed serves to illuminate the engulfing historical crisis which determines the action of the play. In so doing it forces us constantly to re-appraise the position of the hero. Instead of looking at developments through his eyes, at it were, we are driven to question his understanding of himself and of his activities in the light of our wider knowledge of the corporate situation, and to try to relate his subjective sense of value and purpose to his actual influence upon the society of his time. This is something we must look at closely.

What makes Götz such a vital and impressive personality – as most critics would accept – is the unity and coherence of his self-awareness. He does not seem conscious of any tension between his will to self-realisation and his obligations to those with whom he is in contact. His feeling of responsibility to the individuals in his charge or those in need seems to arise out of an immediate awareness of their reality as persons and is as spontaneous as it is whole-hearted (78 ff.; 119 ff.; 127 ff.). His life of ceaseless, vital activity which he pursues with such whole-hearted enjoyment is also a life of service. His quest for self-fulfilment is identical with his desire to help the deprived and helpless.[8] The 'greatness' which Bruder Martin sees in Götz is that of a man who realises in himself all the, 'Kräfte, durch

43

die wir werden, wachsen und gedeihen', whose life, however, is a source of constant personal and communal enrichment (80 f.).

Götz's intuitive and unproblematic sense of relatedness to all he meets — be they neighbours, subordinates, friends or casual acquaintances — is grounded in his deeplying sense of society as an extended family: as a closely integrated, hierarchical structure of relationships held together by mutual affection and respect and by a common feeling of shared loyalties. He looks back with nostalgia at the time when Princes could live in close, co-operative harmony with their subjects and neighbours:

> Sollten wir nicht hoffen ..., daß Verehrung des Kaisers, Fried und Freundschaft der Nachbarn und Lieb der Untertanen der kostbarste Familienschatz sein wird, der auf Enkel und Urenkel erbt? (142)

Society as Götz sees it, is a limitlessly extending network of close interlocking ties. Freedom for him is above all the right of the individual to realise his sense of involvement in society in his own way. In claiming the right to self-help he is asserting his right to rectify injustice whether it is directed against himself or anyone who is defenceless (86 f.; 90 f.; 142 f.). In thus fighting for social justice and unity he is — he constantly assumes — serving the Emperor in a vital and constructive way. He clearly cannot conceive of a situation in which a valid moral response to a human being in need could be at odds with his political duty towards the head of state. Indeed he clearly regards his normal day-to-day life as expressing his devoted service to the Emperor.

There can be no doubt that Goethe is deeply attracted to the moral outlook of Götz and above all to the unity and integrity of his self-awareness. And yet though the dramatist is out to affirm the moral strength of his hero he is also concerned to expose this strength as a limitation. Götz's drive to see all social relationships as personal, moral ties reveals — as Goethe makes clear — a fatal restriction of vision: an inability to see himself and his situation in the perspective of wider historical developments. His longing to restore elementary, patriarchal forms of society exclude him from playing a productive part in the accelerating processes of social change. For the society which is coming into being, as the Emperor sees, is vaster, more complex in organisation and must increasingly be controlled by sophisticated constitutional and political institutions.

The hero's failure to realise this is in the end the cause of his defeat. As we have seen, he is outmanoeuvred and discredited by those who are in control of the effective political and legal agencies of society and can use them against him. But Goethe is saying more than this. Götz's inability to accept a specifically political, corporate order of responsibility does not just expose him to ruthless opponents, it makes him from the very beginning, a disruptive force in the life of society, and that in a way he cannot himself grasp. In reacting as he does to the evils around him he is impeding positive social development. Goethe shows through the sovereign insight of the Emperor that the possibilities of genuine cultural-social progress inherent in this age of transition lie in the bringing of the whole Empire within the authority of a binding, unifying constitutional system. The personalistic moral awareness which is the source of Götz's inner integrity and strength makes him the enemy of Maximilian's aspirations.

This contradiction between moral awareness and political involvement which Götz himself cannot recognise, becomes crucially apparent towards the end of the play when he takes over, albeit for a short time, the leadership of the revolting peasants (159). It is noticeable that Goethe presents this rising simply as an outburst of destructive fury which has no clear political justification or constructive possibility.[9] Götz's readiness to identify himself with it stems primarily from a moral aim – an aim which in itself seems valid. He is not seeking any political break-through but simply to lessen the devastation it is causing, to bring some moderation to what he sees is an unbridled orgy of destruction. But whatever the character of his guiding motives his identification with the peasants is politically disastrous: he is seen to be in open revolt against Maximilian's authority and the established legal and political order of the Empire. The hero's involvement in the Peasants' Revolt marks the occasion of his irrecoverable defeat: it provides his enemies with the opportunity of destroying him finally. But the main significance of this involvement lies – as the dramatist presents it – in its implications for the inward experience of Götz. Here he is overwhelmed by a disabling experience of helplessness – helplessness in the face of the unabated, meaningless orgy of destruction, and helplessness before the pursuing enemies who are totally indifferent to his motives or aims. And out of this cumulative experience of impotence and defeat there grows an awareness of despair which embraces the whole world of history:

45

Und jetzt ist's nicht Weislingen allein, ... nicht der Tod des Kaisers und meine Wunden — es ist alles zusammen. (173)

His deepest moral yearnings, his search for freedom, justice and loyalty, he sees destroyed by the relentless, meaningless forces of history. The spectator, it seems to me, is able to enter sympathetically into the disillusion and despair of Götz, but he also perceives it in a quite different perspective from the hero himself. Götz sees himself as overcome by deceit, treachery and the sheer military power of those who destroy the unity and the harmony of the Empire. His defeat marks the triumph of evil forces which, he foresees, will bring disunity, privation and untold misery to all its peoples. He seems totally overwhelmed by the awareness of a contradiction between his sincere yearning for right, freedom and unity and the blind power of circumstance, between his ideal moral aspiration and the reality of political might. The spectator, while able to share in the intensity of Götz's despair, is able to see it in a wider historical context which, as we have seen, Götz himself cannot fully grasp. In particular, the spectator has to perceive this experience of devouring hopelessness in relation to the Emperor's quest for more enlightened and sophisticated forms of constitutional, legal and social organisation appropriate to the new age which is coming into being — a quest which Götz himself cannot acknowledge, and which his activities actually help to frustrate.

Now this ability to see the defeat of the hero in a broader context forces us to qualify his experience of complete historical futility: to see it as the despair of this isolated individual whose deepest moral longings are shattered by the momentum of historical developments. The play, however, does not stop with the hero's defeat and helplessness. In the final scene as Götz senses the nearing of death, he becomes aware of his rootedness in an order of being which can never be annulled:

Allmächtiger Gott! Wie wohl ist's unter deinem Himmel! Wie frei! — Die Bäume treiben Knospen, und alle Welt hofft. (174)

This awareness of a creative, divinely sustained cosmos releases Götz from hopelessness and enables him to face death as a man reconciled and at peace. In this scene Goethe is evoking dimensions of reality which acquire a decisive dramatic significance, but which seem to have no root in the historical circumstances governing the development of the action. Not surprisingly critics have been puzzled by this discontinuity and have sought in different ways to relate this climactic mystical experience of Götz to the empirical forces which determine his fate.[10] The hero's reconciliation with his lot presupposes, however, that he gives up the search for meaning in history and sees his life as part of an order beyond the reach of its violating, obstructive force.

The problematic character of Götz's experience of redemption lies in my view in the fact that the dramatist who has up till now relativized the self-awareness of the hero, now sees it as the organ of a supreme reality which transcends historical-social processes. Götz who has appeared till this point as a perplexed and largely deluded agent in the treacherous world of history is now seen as achieving a vision of life which raises him above all the other figures and fills him with a redemptive, metaphysical assurance. In this final stage of the action Götz, it seems clear, is removed more and more from the sphere of relative conditioning forces. In his transforming experience of release he is able to look down, as it were, on the great evils which will submerge the nation:

Es kommen die Zeiten des Betrugs, es ist ihm Freiheit gegeben. Die Nichtswürdigen werden regieren mit List, und der Edle wird in ihre Netze fallen. (175)

In its dramatic context it is not possible to see this as the prophecy of an individual who is trapped in an overpowering historical situation he cannot oversee. Goethe invests this vision with the full authority of the hero who has grown beyond the constricting conflicts of history and is now able to see them from the standpoint of a higher religious certainty. In prophesying that the future of the German nation lies in the hands of those who rule by treachery and violence, Götz sees the nation as the stricken, passive hero of another kind of historical tragedy: a tragedy of persisting, meaningless suffering which, as Goethe's contemporaries were aware, still shaped their everyday existence in the late 18th-century.[11] In the play itself it is the Emperor, more than Götz, who personifies this engulfing collective anguish. He it is who pursues the vision of a more humane and unified nation – a vision which is to be shattered by the blind, disregarding lust for power of the Princes. Indeed,

Maximilian's quest for a resolved, harmonious Empire which leads him to reject Götz, makes it easier for the Princes to extend their kingdoms in a way which divides the nation into the unforeseeable future and denies its people all freedom and dignity.

The ending of *Götz von Berlichingen* evokes two different and conflicting kinds of tragic effect. On the one hand, the spectator is drawn to acknowledge the hero's power to transcend the powers which destroy him and to accept his destiny. In Götz's ability to experience his unity with these ultimate forces of life which sustain his being the spectator is able to undergo himself a profound experience of reconciliation. At the same time, however, he must also confront a quite different kind of insight. In the face of the great inescapable suffering which awaits the whole nation he is drawn into an attitude of dissent — a will to reject the arbitrary, despotic systems of government which oppress and bind her people.

The peculiar ambiguity of Götz which has provoked so many contradictory critical responses over the years stems, I think, from the fact that the dramatist seeks to embrace these quite different modes of tragic insight in one dramatic action and is pursuing in fact consciously or unconsciously, two opposing kinds of imaginative effect. In the first place he presents the personal tragedy of Götz who is more and more deeply ensnared and in the end destroyed by the might of historical circumstances which seem to negate all those values impelling his existence. This tragedy culminates in Götz's inner triumph over these destructive forces and in his reconciliation with his fate. It reaches its climax in the revelation of a universe which the spectator can affirm and which transcends all the meaningless, insoluble conflicts of history.

Underlying this personal tragedy, however, is the corporate tragedy of the German nation which is here still in its early stages and extends into a horrifying future far beyond the limits of the stage-action. The problem is that the presuppositions of these two modes of tragedy are not only quite different but inescapably at odds with each other. They stem, it seems, from two quite different views of the agency of the dramatic figures and their place in the world of the play and involve quite conflicting kinds of artistic purpose. Although this collision of creative impulses only becomes fully apparent at the end of *Götz von Berlichingen*, it informs the whole conception of the work. As far as I can see this tense, unresolved confrontation of different kinds of tragic insight and intention is one of the most historically important and influential aspects of the work. This is the source, I suspect, of the peculiar power of the play to grip the imagination of the young writers of the Sturm und Drang and to influence their dramatic endeavours in ways which they were themselves often unable to grasp.

Chapter 3

LENZ AND THE COMEDY

I

Lenz's theoretical preoccupation with Shakespearean tragedy throughout the early 1770's served indirectly to confirm and deepen his creative involvement with the comedy. The pervading sense of a contradiction between the individual and his surroundings which informs his intuitive response to Shakespeare plays was in conflict (I have suggested) with his central convictions about the nature of the tragic form, but it seems to have impelled his search for new and quite revolutionary modes of comedy.[1] In the *Anmerkungen* he was still unable – or unwilling – to confront critically these novel, experimental artistic aims. Shortly before he presented his essay for publication (probably late in 1773) he did, it is true, include a short and rather perfunctory paragraph on comedy. Here he defines the comic form as the structural inversion of the tragic, and in so doing once again openly refutes accepted Aristotelian doctrine:

> Meiner Meinung nach wäre immer der Hauptgedanke einer Komödie, eine Sache, einer Tragödie eine Person. Eine Mißheirat, ein Fündling, irgend eine Grille eines seltsamen Kopfs (die Person darf uns weiter nicht bekannt sein, als insofern ihr Charakter diese Grille, diese Meinung, selbst dieses System veranlaßt haben kann: wir verlangen hier nicht die ganze Person zu kennen) ... Die Personen sind für die Handlungen da – für die artigen Erfolge, Wirkungen, Gegenwirkungen, ein Kreis herumgezogen, der sich um eine Hauptidee dreht – und es ist eine Komödie ... In der Komödie ... gehe ich von den Handlungen aus, und lasse Personen Teil dran nehmen welche ich will. (361)

Despite its rather self-consciously iconoclastic air this definition, as critics have repeatedly pointed out, is deeply rooted in conventional notions of comic situation and character.[2] Commentators, however, have failed to note just how ambiguous it appears in the context of Lenz's argument as a whole. For he is here describing comedy in terms which recall directly his analysis of the debased French pseudo-tragedy which he is out completely do discredit. Comedy – he insists – is a plot-controlled form which demands the strict subordination of character. This implies, it would seem, that comedy (like the French tragedy) is a contrived, arbitrary mode without substantial reality or moral significance.

Lenz does not openly acknowledge this structural kinship but the similarity of his argument in both parts of his essay suggests that he sensed it at some deep intuitive level. Although his aim is to give a dispassionate theoretical definition of comedy as a genre he seems discomfited by its treacherous, equivocal character. This form which seems so deeply bound to the everyday world of social existence – he appears to sense – may in fact trap the playwright in the compulsions of his own subjective imagination. Comedy which lends itself so easily to the close observation of the empirical world may in reality be little more than the vehicle of the fantasies of its creator. This deep-seated unease in Lenz's attitude to comedy is, I think, all the more significant for the fact that he seems unable to recognise it clearly.

It was not until some eighteen months later (in the early months of 1775) that Lenz attempted another fuller discussion of comedy in his review of his own play *Der neue Menoza*. Here his main concern is to emphasize the dependence of comedy as a form on the conditions of the society in which it comes into being:

> Komödie ist Gemälde der menschlichen Gesellschaft, und wenn die ernsthaft wird, kann das Gemälde nicht lachend werden. Daher schrieb Plautus komischer als Terenz, und Moliére komischer als Destouches und Beaumarchais. (419)

As a society becomes more complex and problematic, so (Lenz argues) the exuberant, 'laughing' dimension in comedy declines. In the late 18th-century – and here he is thinking primarily of Beaumarchais – it has become the medium of a questioning, critical awareness of social existence which has more and more excluded the naive laughter and sheer enjoyment of older comic forms. The main function of the genre in contemporary Germany, as Lenz sees it, is enlightening and educative. For of all the dramatic kinds comedy is the only one which is truly 'democratic', able to reach and influence the most unsophisticated social groups which have no understanding of the august vision of tragedy:

Ich nenne durchaus Komödie nicht eine Vorstellung, die bloß Lachen er-
regt, sondern eine Vorstellung, die für jedermann ist. (418)

Lenz is thus concerned to see comedy primarily in the context
of the cultural development of contemporary society, and to regard
it as an essentially provisional form. The purpose of comedy as he
sees it here is to heighten the aesthetic and moral understanding of
the ordinary people in such a way as to make them capable of tragic
experience: it aims to prepare a wide and receptive audience which
can respond as one to the tragedy of the future. Comedy appears in
this perspective as the elementary forerunner of higher tragic forms
which will engage and regenerate the whole nation in some indefi-
nite age to come.

This approach to comedy is clearly quite different from that in
the *Anmerkungen*, but here too, it seems to me, one can sense
Lenz's deeplying disquiet about the comic mode, the same dispa-
raging urge to assert its artistic inferiority to tragedy. He does certainly attribute to modern comedy a serious didactic purpose but
this is essentially transitory and dictated by the cultural divisions
in contemporary society; it is also bound up with what Lenz seems
to see as a basic vulgarity and simplicity inherent in the genre. However much he values the educative possibilities of comedy in late
18th-century Germany his view of himself as 'der deutsche Plautus'
implies an ironic self-abasement before the author of *Götz von
Berlichingen* and *Faust* which (as Lenz clearly recognised) laid claim
here and now to an artistic significance which transcended all local
historical-social circumstances.[3]

Both these discussions of comedy are informed by a deep, unsettling ambivalence which remains essentially unexpressed.
Whether Lenz defines it in terms of an equivocal inversion of tragic
necessity or attributes to it a temporary, socially imposed function,
his considerations of the comedy betray a hesitancy, a will to
qualify and even denigrate its significance which he never articu-
lates. Whenever Lenz speaks of comedy he tends, almost instinctively, so see it in the light of an absence or failure of tragedy, or of
tragedy's unattainability or loss.

When we turn to Lenz's plays themselves we can see at once
why critics have generally regarded them as a special kind of tragi-
comedy.[4] Our discussion of his theoretical statements on comedy
should prepare us, however, for works which are, I believe, more

53

ambiguous, disjointed and sheerly disconcerting than we have yet begun to grasp.

II

Lenz probably began working on *Der neue Menoza* in 1773 although it was not completed till the following year. The genesis of the work thus overlaps with that of *Der Hofmeister* which was begun even earlier but not completed until the same year.[5] Both plays in their different ways represent highly idiosyncratic attempts to explore new, innovative modes of comedy which left many of Lenz's contemporaries deeply perplexed and which still today provoke serious critical dispute.[6]

At the centre of the action in *Der neue Menoza* is the figure of Prince Tandi, who during his tour of Europe makes the acquaintance of the Biederling family. He falls in love with their daughter Wilhelmine and eventually marries her. Not long after the wedding, however, Herr von Zopf, who has been for many years on assignments for Biederling in Italy, turns up with the news that Tandi (as he has heard from the Jesuits) is in fact the long lost son of the Biederlings, and that Tandi and Wilhelmine are in fact brother and sister (145). This revelation thrusts the lovers into deep uncomprehending despair. But after some time Babet, Wilhelmine's former nurse, suddenly confesses that unknown to everyone she is Wilhelmine's real mother (169 f.). This new revelation means that the marriage is legitimate, that the lovers are not guilty of incest and that they can enter once more into their original state of supreme happiness.

In the course of the play Wilhelmine and Tandi are exposed to violent reversals of fortune. From pure untroubled joy they are thrown suddenly into hopelessness, only to be just as unpredictably rescued by Babets' restoring confession. These reversals show the complete helplessness of the lovers in the face of incalculable revelations. The comic character of the play depends crucially on the timing of these disclosures. The shattering force of Zopf's revelation stems from the fact that it comes after the lovers have consummated their union, while the saving force of Babets' confession depends on the fact that it comes before the experience of despair has led, as seems inevitable for a time, to self-destruction. But though the timing of these revelations is crucial, it is noticeable that Lenz does not attempt to make them seem probable, to integrate them into a clear process of dramatic motivation. Zopf simply reappears out of the blue after many years of absence while Babet just as suddenly reveals the secret she has hugged to herself since Wilhelmine's birth. Lenz seems intent on stressing the unaccountable, eruptive character of both events. The dramatic situation, he seems to be showing, is not fixed or lucid; it bears within it hidden forces of disruption which neither the dramatic characters nor the spectator suspect. The individual's sense of his identity can be shattered in a moment and he can be stripped of his closest relationships without warning. Yet despite the volatility and confusion of this situation the action leads neatly to its appointed resolution; it stands out as a controlling, purposive structure in a haphazard impenetrable world. Lenz seems concerned to emphasize ironically this discrepancy between the dramatic situation and the development of the plot – to suggest that the action does not grow inevitably out of the situation but is rather imposed upon it. He seems in fact intent on highlighting the arbitrarily contrived character of the whole dramatic development. This is most evident in the destructive way he counterposes tragic and comic insights in the action in order to show that though his play aspires to embrace comic and tragic significances, it fails to achieve either.

Lenz intends to show that after Zopf's revelation Tandi and Wilhelmine do undergo an experience of genuine tragic dereliction. Tandi in particular is aware of confronting a world which contradicts his deepest moral impulses and forces upon him a terrible guilt he has not willed (174 f.). However, this 'tragic' experience, it soon turns out, is all a mistake: it has no relation to Tandi's actual situation as Babets' confession makes quite clear. But although this confession exposes the spuriousness of the 'tragic' anguish, the shattering awareness of the randomness of events which has seized the lovers, equally undermines the 'comic' resolution. For this, dependent as it is on an accident of timing, merely reflects in another form the final contingency of things. The lovers can be neither genuinely tragic victims nor real comic survivors, since they must always be aware of being at the mercy of arbitrary, unaccountable circumstance.

Lenz thus seems at pains to demonstrate that the world the play brings to life precludes any valid resolution, comic or tragic. He has, he implies, brought the action to a happy end but it might as well have ended in catastrophe; the difference between the two lies in the chance timing of the decisive revelation and this, like all dramatic accidents, is at the playwright's discretion. The fact that he has designed this particular 'willkürlicher Tanz' as opposed to another depends upon his own subjective inclination, and this too is unaccountable.

In *Der Hofmeister* it seems that Lenz is attempting to create a completely different comic structure. The action does not depend upon secret events in the past but arises directly out of a particular, recognizable social situation and is conceived analytically. The dramatic developments are determined by two sets of interacting social tensions: tensions between the middle-class tutor and the two aristocratic von Berg families which control his position, and the tensions between parent and child in both upper- and middle-class families. Lenz traces the profound effect of these forces on the dramatic figures and seems to adopt the stance of a sardonic, detached observer. He is concerned to present the three young people at the centre of the action – Läuffer the tutor, Gustchen the daughter of Major von Berg, and Fritz, son of his brother, the Geheimrat – as the victims of impersonal determinants whose working can be analysed and assessed by empirical means.

Lenz makes it clear that each of the three young protagonists is caught up in a crisis which stems directly from decisions made in the parental generation. Near the beginning of the play the Geheimrat takes the decisive step of separating Gustchen and Fritz who are childhood sweethearts, by denying them the possibility of any contact or even private correspondence during Fritz's time at university (23 f.). This has the effect of imprisoning Gustchen in particular in a life of stifling loneliness and frustration. The social ambitions of her parents deny her any relationship with girls of her own age and she comes more and more to seek compensation in the inner world of her adolescent imagination (40).

Läuffer too is trapped in a life of corroding frustration. He comes to Insterburg in the hope of gaining the patronage which would help him find a professional position but finds in fact that it is a dead end (27). He has to accept increasingly drastic cuts in salary and to realize that the possibilities of travel he has been promised are denied him. Moreover, he soon realizes that the Major and his wife are quite indifferent to the instruction he gives their children (16 ff.); that they indeed consistently treat him as a servant who has no right to his own judgements. At the same time Läuffer recognizes only too clearly that his own father, the Pastor, is unable or unwilling to provide the financial help which would help him break free.

The crucial sexual encounter between Gustchen and Läuffer, as Lenz presents it, is completely devoid of passion. It is rather a conjunction of two lonely, suffering beings each trapped in his own misery and seeking compulsively for some kind of release. Lenz emphasizes this by recurrent ironic references to great tragic love-affairs. When Gustchen addresses Läuffer as Romeo she is thinking not of him but the absent Fritz, or to be more precise, of an idealized fantasy of the lover she has lost:

> O Romeo! wenn dies deine Hand wäre – aber so verlässest du mich, unedler Romeo! Siehst nicht, daß deine Julie für dich stirbt – von der ganzen Welt, von ihrer ganzen Familie gehaßt, verachtet, ausgespien. *(Drückt seine Hand an ihre Augen.)* (41)

Similarly when Läuffer identifies himself with Abelard this betrays not profound passion but a disabling fear – fear of the consequences for himself which may flow from this breach of accepted morality (41). The mututal estrangement of the two lovers becomes fully apparent when their union is discovered. Each flees in self-enclosing terror, separately and in opposite directions. Lenz thus presents this sexual encounter ironically as the symptom of emotional exposure and confusion. In giving themselves to each other Gustchen and Läuffer are both yielding to compulsions which neither recognizes or understands but which drive them helplessly onwards towards consequences they cannot foresee.

The crises which overtake Gustchen, Läuffer and, in a different way, Fritz in his life at University in Halle, are the direct consequence of parental attitudes and decisions. Each of the parents pursues his own individual ends and these often seem to have little in common. But Lenz aims to show at work in these apparently separate aims the determining pressure of a class-awareness which links the individual figures in ways they themselves cannot understand. This is very evident in the dramatist's presentation of the two von

57

Berg brothers. The idealistic Geheimrat seems at first sight to have little in common with his socially aspiring, eccentric brother. In fact, it is the Geheimrat who exposes the emptiness of the Major's social ambitions. He shows how the latter's desire for a private tutor is not rooted in educational concern but in a competitive will to make his home into a court – a will intensified by the subservience of the middle-class tutors:

> Wer ist schuld daran, als ihr Schurken von Hauslehrern? Würde der Edelmann nicht von euch in der Grille gestärkt, einen kleinen Hof anzulegen, wo er als Monarch oben auf dem Thron sitzt und ihm Hofmeister und Mamsell und ein ganzer Wisch von Tagdieben huldigen, so würd er seine Jungen in die öffentliche Schule tun müssen. (28 f.)

The Geheimrat is, however, quite unable to see the determining class-pressures at work in his own behaviour. On the two occasions when he intervenes decisively in the dramatic action, his motives, as Lenz makes clear, are more complex and equivocal than he himself believes.[7]

It is the Geheimrat who rejects Läuffer's application for the teaching-post at the village school and who thus serves to trap him irrevocably at Insterburg (11). The Geheimrat claims that he rejects the tutor out of a disinterested concern for high academic standards and there is no doubt that such concern ist very important to him. But it is equally true, as Läuffer bitterly points out, that the Geheimrat is insisting on intellectual abilities quite out of keeping with the actual position, and that he regards Läuffer in any case with a condescension which flows from arrogant disregard of the tutor's true predicament. The Geheimrat sees Läuffer's difficulties as a result of personal fecklessness: he sees him as remaining passively content with a position which he could choose to reject. This inability to understand Läuffer's position betrays a class-conditioned blindness. As Pastor Läuffer discreetly suggests, the Geheimrat is unable to grasp from his own position of aristocratic privilege the harsh economic realities determining his son's predicament and thus attributes to innate weakness difficulties over which the tutor has no control (27). In the Geheimrat's high-handed dismissal of Läuffer the dramatist exposes an impulse of class-arrogance which Berg himself cannot acknowledge. His pedagogic idealism is ambiguously bound up with a will to direct and control – to create the village-school in the image of his own lofty concerns – which, Lenz suggests, is grounded in his pre-eminent social position.

This ambiguity in the Geheimrat's behaviour is perhaps even more evident in his treatment of his son Fritz. His harsh suppression of Fritz's relationship with Gustchen is in ironic contrast to his rhetorically expressed belief that freedom is the condition of the individual's spiritual growth and fulfilment (25). Here and later in his ready acceptance of Seiffenblase's malicious reports of Fritz's behaviour, Lenz is exposing an imperious drive in the Geheimrat's behaviour which contradicts his view of himself as an enlightened thinker who transcends class-attitudes and interests. The dramatist is at pains to point up this discrepancy between the rôle of the Geheimrat as a *raisonneur* who exposes aristocratic arrogance and vanity and embraces the ideal of a harmonious, integrated society, and his function as a dramatic agent whose behaviour frequently betrays just those conditioned, destructive responses he rhetorically condemns. Like the other aristocratic figures in the play he is impelled by an inborn assumption of superiority and will to dominance which are deeply rooted in his class-identity.

Lenz thus presents the dramatic crises in *Der Hofmeister* in a subtly ironic perspective. He enables the spectator to see determining forces at work in all the different relationships which the protagonists themselves cannot recognize. His aim is to show that these figures who are so at odds with one another, are in fact caught up in a seemingly all-embracing and irresistible process of social determination. Where the characters are aware only of mutual separation and estrangement, Lenz enables the spectator to see the fateful operation of environmental constraints which drive the dramatic agents nearer and nearer to disaster. Both Gustchen and Läuffer in their different situations are consumed by guilt and deepening self-hatred. She, convinced that she is responsible for her father's death, tries to drown herself (64 f.; 69). Läuffer, believing that Gustchen is dead, castrates himself in bitter remorse (80). Meanwhile Fritz, who has been rejected by his father and is still shackled by his friend Pätus' debts, also learns with horror of Gustchen's death (85). In each case it is a misunderstanding which threatens to precipitate an irreversible disaster and Lenz is clearly concerned to present these misunderstandings as the consequence and symptom of profound inner confusion: as the clinching revelation of a victimisation at the hands of society before which the individual is defenceless.

59

And yet none of these crises leads to catastrophe. The three main figures are rescued against all the odds and quite unpredictably. At the very moment when she throws herself in the pond Gustchen is seen by her father who saves her (69); Läuffer is rescued from despair by a girl, Lise, who appears out of the blue and who loves him for himself despite his disabilities (93 ff.); Pätus has a great win on the lottery which enables Fritz and himself to return home, overcome all the misunderstandings and renew their emotional commitments (88 f.). In each case a stroke of incalculable good fortune brings a seemingly disastrous situation to a happy conclusion. Up to this point in the action Lenz has traced the unfolding of accountable processes of social causation. Now all of a sudden he shows how these processes can be suspended and reversed by unpredictable developments. The seeming inevitability of the catastrophic momentum yields to an irresistible impetus to comic reconciliation. Lenz goes out of his way to emphasize the fortuitous and arbitrary character of this resolution which hangs on the conjunction of three equally unforeseeable and improbable events at just the right time. He obviously wants the spectator to share with Pätus the feeling that he has left behind the world of social antagonisms and privations and entered a sphere in which circumstances are in complete accord with the individual's deepest desires:

> Bin ich so glücklich? oder ist's nur ein Traum? ein Rausch? — eine Bezauberung? (99).

To grasp the comic character of *Der Hofmeister* we have to respond to this sharp disjunction between analysable social processes and the contrivances which make possible the comic ending. Lenz seems to be ironically proclaiming that this *dénouement* does not grow out of the preceding dramatic developments but is violently forced upon them — and in a way which emphasizes its contradiction of what has gone before. Throughout most of the first four acts of the play Lenz presents the victimization of the characters as a subjection to the impersonal power of society which seems to acquire a malevolent, fateful force. In the final scenes, however, he shows that the compulsion which he has analysed in the working of social processes is not an irreversible, tragic necessity but prone, like other contingent forces, to the intrusion of unforeseeable eventualities. The social processes which had seemed to form an irresistible tragic momentum are now exposed as lacking final necessity. They do not enable that self-transcending awareness which the dramatist in Lenz's view experiences only in the face of supreme, metaphysical reality. In overriding the seemingly compelling processes of social causation, he seems to be exposing the contingency of the dramatic world – his inability as an observer to find any ultimate principle of moral significance. Once again his aim is apparently to query the coherence of the dramatic action by drawing attention to himself as the manipulating choreographer who capriciously uses coincidence to shape developments in accordance with his own subjective inclinations. The arbitrary, hollow comic ending reveals the failure of the dramatist to perceive a finally binding order in the world of the play which could find embodiment in a necessary aesthetic structure. The degeneration of the closely observed analysis of a social situation into an absurd, clichéed and inadequate comic resolution is the grotesque symbol of this failure.

III

In both *Der neue Menoza* and *Der Hofmeister* Lenz counterposes tragic and comic impulses as a means of emphasizing ironically the arbitrary, incoherent character of the dramatic form. The comic impetus in both works involves a pointing up of the gap between an intractable, random world and a contrived dramatic structure without organic necessity or expressive significance. This tension between tragic and comic insights also pervades the conception of *Die Soldaten*, Lenz's last major play.[8] Here, however, he makes a new and far-reaching attempt to hold these conflicting tendencies together in close, discordant interaction in his perception of the tensely unfolding dramatic developments. Lenz attempts here to realize a conception of the inherently twofold, tragi-comic character of the experience and agency of the protagonists which, it seems to me, is both innovative and prophetic.

As in *Der Hofmeister* Lenz here derives the shaping impulses of the action from a particular, observable social situation. In the relations between Marie Wesener, her middle-class fiancé Stolzius, and the predatory aristocratic officer, Desportes, Lenz lays bare deeplying antagonisms which drive the characters into a conflict they themselves do not seek and cannot anticipate. In *Die Soldaten*, however, Lenz is much more concerned to explore the hidden ambiguous depths in the experience of these points, ordinary figures. Certainly, he does explore their exposure to environmental pressures in rigorous, probing detail but he is also at pains to show the power of hidden impulses and longings which go beyond their immediate social experience. The characters who appear in one perspective as the hapless objects of social determinants appear in another as intense, aspiring agents in their own right. Lenz presents the two main middle-class figures in particular in this disconcertingly two-fold way.

At first sight the playwright seems intent on realising an ironically diagnostic view of Stolzius' relationship with Marie. He makes it clear that the draper's infatuation is bound up with idealized notions of innocence and purity which are rooted in Stolzius' moralistic middle-class background but which have little relevance to this vain, scheming girl he actually wants to marry (211). Similarly, in all his attempts to assert his love for Marie Stolzius appears as the victim of conditioning social pressures.[9] When, for instance, he hears rumours of Marie's relationship with Desportes he turns instinctively to his upper-class acquaintances (Desportes' colleagues) for help and advice (197 ff.). Even in his anguish his responses remain those of the middle-class tradesman who throughout his life has been economically dependent on his aristocratic clientèle. However great love for Marie, it cannot free him from the constricting inhibitions of his subordinate social position.

Yet despite this deterministic analysis of the behaviour of Stolzius the dramatist is also concerned to show his capacity for passionate commitment which is quite incongruous with his everyday responses. There is an agony in his yearnings for Marie which threatens to unhinge his mind but which he cannot translate into consistent purposive action. He is able to act only when he has lost her and has nothing more to lose (240 ff.).

Lenz seeks to portray Marie in the same disjointed way as both a conditioned social being and an aspiring heroine. From one point of view she appears as a coquettish, middle-class girl driven by a conventional ambition to rise in society, to become a 'gnädige Frau' (197). She seems the victim of a vanity which is banal and self-deluded and as such essentially comic. But Lenz also reveals in this conventional longing an impelling vitality which rebels against the suffocating constriction of her narrow middle-class existence and seeks a richer fulfilment. In staking everything on her love for Desportes she is (as the Gräfin de la Roche informs her) setting herself up against the accepted order of society:

> Und Sie glaubten die einzige Person auf der Welt zu sein, die ihn trotz des Zorns seiner Eltern, trotz des Hochmuts seiner Familie, trotz seines Schwurs, trotz seines Charakters, trotz der ganzen Welt treu erhalten wollten? Das heißt, Sie wollten die Welt umkehren. (227)

Underlying her predictable, commonplace hopes there is a force of yearning which, Lenz shows, rejects compromise or acceptance and which drives her relentlessly on despite repeated disappointments. Her love for Desportes may embody a vulgar, materialistic ambition but it also betrays a quest for a freer, more abundant life which in her confined social position she can only identiy with the more commanding and elegant life of the aristocracy.

In his presentation of the unfolding dramatic action Lenz also enforces this diverse contradictory way of seeing. He emphasizes the quickening movement of events towards catastrophe in a manner which suggests that developments are impelled by some inherent tragic inevitability. But at the same time he is at pains to disconcert this sense of necessary progression by interposing episodic scenes which both disrupt its impetus and limit its importance. These scenes portray the corporate life of the officers as they attempt to find diversion from the tedium of peace-time existence and it is noticeable that Lenz places them at crucial points in the development of the main action – at those points where the spectator is becoming most involved in the destinies of the main figures.[10] Each time Lenz shows the officers carrying out a pointless, sadistic joke on a helpless victim (209 f.; 234 ff.; cf. also 216 f.); and each time it is essentially the same joke. Through emphasizing this repetiveness Lenz seems to be drawing attention to the ongoing continuum of ordinary existence and in this way placing the main dramatic events in the context of a wider world which is indifferent to them and largely unaffected by them. His aim, in other words, is to force us to see the subordinate status of the dramatic action. It has no climactic, epitomising significance; it merely represents one series of developments alongside the countless others which make up the day-to-day life of society as a whole.

This attempt to reduce sardonically the impact of the main action is most obvious in Lenz's presentation of the ending of the play, or rather endings, for there are in fact three separate conclusions. One strand of development ends in Stolzius' revenge on Desportes. The cheated lover murders his rival and takes his own life. Lenz contrives both to emphasize the potentially tragic power of these acts of destruction and to deprive them of all tragic significance. He stresses the futility of this revenge, which is impelled by an obsessed fantasy of Marie as a pure and innocent victim and which is in any case of no practical help to her since she is no longer in contact with Desportes (239 ff.). At the same time Lenz also exposes the inherent grotesqueness of this belated act of self-assertion. It is only when he can feel the poison he has taken working within him that Stolzius finally overcomes the subjection to his aristocratic superiors which has prevented him throughout from effectively pressing his claim on Marie. Only now, when he need not face the consequences, is he capable of rebelling against his ingrained submissiveness and striking back at his tormentors. This catastrophe, Lenz forces us to see, has no reconciling tragic power. It has no impact on the life of Marie, no influence on the wider life of society, and it is, moreover, at once driven from the forefront of our attention. In the very next scene the dramatist portrays the reunion and reconciliation of Marie and her father.

This reconciliation evokes the possibility of a new hope and a new beginning and thus seems to conform to conventional notions of a comic resolution.[11] Marie has not died, as her father feared (234 f.); she has not yielded to the temptation to kill herself, nor has she fallen prey to the violence of Desportes' Jäger (240). Her father, despite the horror of bankruptcy, humiliation and the collapse of his secure middle-class world, has also survived and is concerned only about the well-being of his lost daughter (243). This reunion marks the triumph of the relationship between father and daughter over terrible adversity; it shows the unsuspected resilience of their love for each other. Yet Lenz also undermines this hope of a new beginning by showing the social exposure of Marie. She has survived, but what kind of life awaits her now that her family is ruined and ostracised and she has lost her good name? (244). Is she doomed to drag out her existence in the hospice for socially rejected women? What can the love of her father and the sympathy of the Gräfin and the financial help of the Colonel achieve in the face of the rejection of society? Lenz thus contrives to call in question the seemingly positive meaning of this climactic reconciliation. He draws the spectator into a position where he must feel relief and apprehension, hope and misgivings at one and the same time.

The final scene of the play enacts a third ending in which the Colonel of Desportes' regiment and the Gräfin de la Roche discuss ways of preventing a recurrence of the suffering which the Wesener family has undergone. The Colonel puts forward the proposal that a state-brothel staffed by volunteers should be set up as a means of deflecting the predatory sexual energies of the soldiers from respectable middle-class families. Lenz seems at first sight to be trying to temper our awareness of present suffering by anticipating reforms which will prevent such anguish and waste in the future. It soon becomes clear, however, that here too he is out to deny the spectator a positive and coherent response. Though the Colonel does not abandon his proposal, it is clear from the Gräfin's response that it is improbable that it could be realized in the present state of society. Still more fundamental, however, is the fact that this proposal addresses itself only to the symptom of a social disorder and not to its cause. Lenz has taken great pains throughout the play to demonstrate that the irresponsible, aggressive sexuality of the officers is rooted in the exploitative class-outlook of the aristocracy which sees its social pre-eminence as justification for its will to use socially inferior groups as the means of its own pleasure or enrichment. Even if a 'Pflanzenschule' could be successfully established, it could not affect the deep contradictions which pervade the existence of society and underlie the strife and disruption we have observed.

IV

In the *Anmerkungen übers Theater* Lenz defines the comic form in terms which recall the deterministic French tragedy which he condemns as a blasphemous rejection of Providence (357 ff.). It is revealing to compare these passages of the *Anmerkungen* with his description of life in contemporary society at the beginning of his discussion of *Götz von Berlichingen*:

Wir werden geboren — unsere Eltern geben uns Brot und Kleid — unsere
Lehrer drücken in unser Hirn Worte, Sprachen, Wissenschaften — irgend
ein artiges Mädchen drückt in unser Herz den Wunsch es eigen zu besitzen,
... es entsteht eine Lücke in der Republik wo wir hineinpassen — Unsere
Freunde, Verwandte, Gönner setzen an und stoßen uns glücklich hinein —
wir drehen uns eine Zeitlang in diesem Platz herum wie die andern Räder
und stoßen und treiben — bis wir wenn's noch so ordentlich geht abge-
stumpft sind und zuletzt wieder einem neuen Rade Platz machen müssen —
das ist, meine Herren! ohne Ruhm zu melden unsere Biographie — und was
bleibt nun der Mensch noch anders als eine vorzüglich-künstliche kleine
Maschine, die in die große Maschine, die wir Welt, Weltbegebenheiten,
Weltläufe nennen besser oder schlimmer hineinpaßt. (378)

The awareness of contingency deeply informs, it seems to me,
the conception of Lenz's comedies. He negotiates this, however, not
as a dispassionate observer but as a playwright who is morally and
theologically committed to a belief in Providence and who as a
literary theorist asserts the supremacy of the tragic form.

In Lenz's comedies the action exists in sharp tension to an enclosing world which overshadows it and threatens to rob it of significance. In *Der neue Menoza* the ironic thrust of his comic perception is to play up the discrepancy between the plot which leads to
happiness and reconciliation and the intractable reality of a world
which denies it any moral or aesthetic meaning. The union of the
lovers far from revealing the beneficent nature of things just con-
firms from another point of view the ultimate absurdity of an existence in which suffering and joy are alike the result of a blind conjunction of accidental forces. The 'providential' release of the protagonists from (wholly unmerited) guilt and despair is brought
about, it seems, only by the intervention of the dramatist who
against all the odds imposes a positive, reassuring order on a world
without any discernible design or purpose.

In *Der Hofmeister* the playwright emphasizes this same incon-
gruence between the comic development and the impenetrable
randomness of life. Here again the happy-ending arises out of a
situation of seemingly irreversible disruption. In the first part of the
play Lenz lays bare a crisis which is inherent in the social dependence of the characters — a dependence which they themselves cannot recognise. He thus enables the spectator to perceive a coherent
accelerating process of conflict and to sense the imminence of a
catastrophe which seems inescapable.

66

However, as we have seen, this process is suspended by the irruption of three incalculable and completely unforeseeable developments in the different strands of the action. These transform the position of the three young protagonists at a stroke; all of them find themselves overtaken by a happiness they could not have dreamt of just shortly before.

Lenz seems concerned to show that the processes of social determination he lays bare with such probing care constitute a kind of necessity — a necessity which is coherent and compelling and which moreover can be demonstrated by empirical, scientific means. All of a sudden, however, he drops this rigorous, analytical standpoint and seems intent on showing precisely that the social dependence of the characters is not inescapable, that it is not in fact a tragic necessity at all. It is as if he wants to prove that he as a dramatist is not bound by it; that he enjoys the freedom to break the hold of environmental forces over his characters and release them from disaster. His instrusive use of the well-tried, unmotivated devices of a conventional comedy is the means by which he suspends the processes of social causation and asserts his sovereignty as the choreographer who arranges things according to his desires. But, as in *Der neue Menoza*, the effect of this wishful *dénouement* serves only to emphasizes the intractable otherness of the alien, oppressive world of society which seems bent on denying all man's in-born intuitions of order and value.

In *Die Soldaten* Lenz realises a quite different kind of comic conception which seems much more in keeping with inherited notions of dramatic progression and coherence. Here he is not out to intrude ironically upon the development of the action, to distort its shaping impetus. His aim is rather to realise the unfolding tensions which are inherent in the relationship of the heroine with her two competing suitors and are clearly apparent in the very first scenes of the play.

Yet in *Die Soldaten* too the playwright seems in a different, more subtle way just as intent on questioning the character and status of the action. Here, however, the dramatic developments are not — as in his earlier works — in confrontation with the wider world of the play. They are problematic rather because they are of a kind with it and reflect its pervading ambiguity. Lenz presents the action in *Die Soldaten* as a sequence of events among the countless others within the ceaseless continuum of social existence, and

67

portrays them in a way which deprives them of any climactic force or significance. He places the action in an ironically shifting perspective which evokes at times the resonance of tragedy while denying it all genuine cathartic effect, which frequently mimics the renewing movement of comedy without generating real comic release. Lenz seems to emphasize this impenetrable opaqueness throughout. He takes the dramatic events from the day-to-day life of society and to this extent asserts their reality, but he seems quite unable interpret them. He is at a loss, it appears, to say why he selects them and so lends them priority over other developments he neglects, since they (presumably like these developments too) are throughout open to quite contradictory interpretations and assessments. The fragmented, inconclusive ending of the play appears as the final confirmation of this insoluble ambiguity. Not only is the dramatist at pains to expose the apparently 'tragic' and 'comic' conclusions as grotesque, self-deflating parodies; he is also concerned to suggest that his quite seriously intended proposal for reform (put forward in the original version by no lesser person than the Gräfin herself[12]) may be equally futile and absurd.

This is the context in which we must see Lenz's attempts to use his comedies as an instrument of effective social criticism and reform. He was, as Georg Büchner clearly saw, a man deeply sensitive to the suffering of the deprived and the helpless[13], and there can be no doubt that he took his mission as critic and reformer very seriously. This is very clearly expressed, for instance, in his letter to Herder to whom he had sent a copy of *Die Soldaten*, in November 1775:

> Ich freue mich himmlische Freude, daß Du mein Stück gerade von der Seite empfindest auf der ichs empfunden wünschte, von der Politischen. Doch es konnte nicht fehlen, überall auf deine Meynungen und Grundsätze gepfropft.[14]

His letter to the real Gräfin de la Roche, to whom he also commended *die Soldaten*, explains much more fully how he conceived the social-moral purpose of his plays:

> So ist denn dieser Nerve des Gefühls bey Ihnen auch angeschlagen. Könnten aber Personen von Ihrem Stande, Ihren Einsichten, Ihrem Herzen, sich jemals ganz in den Gesichtskreis dieser Armen herabniedrigen, anschauend

wie Gott erkennen, was ihnen Kummer, der oft mit einer Handbewegung
eines erleuchteten Wesens wie der Stein von dem Grabe Christi weggewälzt
werden könnte, auf die Ihnen eigenthümliche Art behandeln. Ach! das
große Geheimnis, sich in viele Gesichtspunkte zu stellen, und jeden Menschen mit seinen Augen ansehen zu können! Sie wären die erste Frau von
Stande, die das gefühlt hätte! ... Sie sollten einmal ein Stück von mir lesen:
Die Soldaten. Überhaupt wird meine Bemühung dahin gehen, die Stände
darzustellen, wie sie sind: nicht, wie sie Personen aus einer höheren Sphäre
sich vorstellen, und den mitleidigen, gefühlvollen, wohltätigen Gottesher-
zen unter diesen neuen Ansichten und Laufbahnen für ihre Göttlichkeit zu
eröffnen. [15]

Lenz's view of the social purpose of his comedies as expressed
here is very close to that which Mercier attributes to the *drame*.
This involves in both cases a realistic concern to show the nature of
existence in the different social groups as it actually is, and in so
doing to overcome prejudice and mutual estrangement. In *Die Soldaten* specifically he is seeking to reveal to rather remote, but potentially well-meaning and concerned members of the aristocracy
the suffering of the vulnerable and lowly in society which usually
goes unnoticed. In this way Lenz – like Mercier – aims to evoke a
sympathy which he feels to be latent but still largely thwarted by
ignorance and indifference. At the same time his presentation of the
figures of the Gräfin de la Roche and Eisenhardt, the army chap-
lain, makes it clear that this is a two-way process. By showing the
caring involvement of these benevolent members of the upper-
classes Lenz is obviously out to counteract the sense of privation
and resentment which pervades the attitude of many members of
the bourgeoisie towards their social superiors.

There can be no doubt, however, that Lenz (again like Mercier)
sees the final purpose of reconciliation as entailing the indictment
of what he sees as the wide-spread evils infecting the life of German
society in the 1770's.

In all his plays he is clearly intent on exposing the arrogance,
greed and cruelty of the aristocracy as a social class in their dealings
with their subordinates. His presentation of the anguish of the
derided, impotent tutor in *Der Hofmeister* was based upon his own
direct experience – and that of many of his friends – as a private
tutor in an aristocratic family. [16] Similarly, the portrayal of the
helpless exposure of Stolzius and other defenceless, victimised figures, like Aaron and Frau Bischof, to the self-indulgent sadism of

the officers was clearly informed by the conviction that such suffering was both very wide-spread and almost completely ignored.

Lenz's analysis of the behaviour of the aristocratic figures in these plays is very radical, however, and seems to me to go far beyond the moralistic perception of playwrights like Mercier. In the portrayal of these characters he seeks to show the working of an inarticulate force of class-awareness which underlies and distorts their conscious understanding of themselves. This is for Lenz the source of that seemingly innate and almost impersonal feeling of detached superiority which drives the nobleman to see himself as existing essentially outside society and, as thus entitled to use it, its laws and agencies and those within it, as the means of his own self-realisation and enjoyment.[17] The behaviour of the aristocrat (as Lenz seeks to demonstrate) is domineering and exploitative, in ways which he as an individual cannot really recognise.

Lenz is also concerned to show up the failings of the middle-class in an equally sardonic and critical way. Here too he lays bare the pressures of an inherent group-awareness which the individual is unable to penetrate fully. At the heart of the experience of the middle-class person, as Lenz sees it, is an unquestioning sense of a dependence on the aristocracy which pervades all his reactions — not least when he is out to proclaim his class-pride and independence. He lays bare this filial helplessness most clearly in the behaviour of figures like Läuffer and Stolzius. He shows how, whenever they find themselves trapped in overwhelming difficulties, they turn reflexively to their upper-class 'benefactors' who to them embody an ultimate sustaining power and authority but who are in reality the source of their predicament.[18] Wesener in the same way senses as if by instinct that the only hope of a fuller, more eminent life lies in the assimilation of his family into the aristocracy through the marriage of his daughter to an upper-class officer. Marie's determination to marry Desportes is thus in fact (as the Gräfin seems to sense)[19] the overt expression of a fantasy which her father has never till now dared to admit even to himself.

This critical analysis of class-attitudes in Lenz's comedies is specific and precise, but very limited in scope. His aim is to change the attitudes of the different social groups to one another within the existing class-structure of contemporary society. He does not seek to abolish this structure but to humanise it: to overcome the prejudice and antagonism which warp the relationships between the classes and prevent individuals separated by social rank from experiencing their common, inseparable involvement in the total life of society and the mutual obligations this entails. In this respect his purpose does not seem so different from that of Mercier and the dramatic theorists of the Enlightenment.[20]

When we approach Lenz's work from this point of view I think we can sense at once a sharp tension between the moral confidence impelling his reformist intentions and the actual working of his creative imagination. Lenz's comedies express a quite new and haunting awareness of the extreme vulnerability of the individual in contemporary society, his helplessness before dark, impersonal forces in himself and in his surroundings which thwart his self-understanding and estrange him from his deepest emotional energies. As a reformer he seems constantly to presume that the individual is capable of moral renewal, of gaining control of his own life and that of his environment. As a playwright, however, it is always the helplessness of the harried, divided self which fires his creative interest; his real imaginative concern is to cut through the apparent order and stability of the lives of his characters and reveal their drivenness in an overwhelming and impenetrable world.

This discrepancy in the conception of Lenz's comedies is most obviously apparent in his deeply ambivalent presentation of the raisonneur – figures – concerned, upper-class individuals who frequently express views very dear to the dramatist, but who are conspicuously unsuccessful in translating their concern into effective action. In *Der Hofmeister*, for instance, the Geheimrat's statements on personal freedom, class-arrogance and education reflect ideas which Lenz himself articulated on other occasions. Yet, as we have seen, the playwright is intent on emphasizing his failure to understand the predicament of the three young people whose lives he seeks to control. Indeed it is his interventions which (as Lenz ironically demonstrates) precipitate the conjunction of events that sweep the young protagonists to the very brink of disaster.

This ambivalence also informs in a more subtle way Lenz's portrayal of the two, more sympathetic, moral idealists in *Die Soldaten*, the Gräfin de la Roche and Eisenhardt, the army-chaplain. Despite his obviously very positive general view of these figures and their well-meaning aims Lenz once again stresses their failure to confront the full complexity of the situation in which they seek to intervene. Both clearly foresee the possibility of a terrible catastrophe but are in the end unable to prevent developments from taking their course.

Eisenhardt, for his part, seems to be speaking for the dramatist when he rejects the officers' attempt to justify their seduction of middle-class girls on the grounds that (as they claim) only 'disreputable' girls succumb to their deceptions:

> ... erlauben Sie mir, Ihnen zu sagen, eine Hure wird niemals eine Hure, wenn sie nicht dazu gemacht wird. Der Trieb ist in allen Menschen, aber jedes Frauenzimmer weiß, daß sie dem Triebe ihre ganze künftige Glückseligheit zu danken hat, und wird sie die aufopfern, wenn man sie nicht drum betrügt? (192)

But although Eisenhardt clearly sees the predatory nature of the officers' sexuality he has no real insight into its deeper causes. This is evident in the way he appeals to the sense of honour of the individual officer – to his *esprit de corps* – for a change of heart. For, as Lenz makes quite clear, it is precisely the inherited, corporate image of the virile, uninhibited officer which stimulates and legitimizes this ruthless will to seduction – a will which in any case just expresses in an extreme form the fundamentally exploitative attitude of the aristocracy to the lower social orders.[21]

In his presentation of the figure of the Gräfin this contradiction in Lenz's attitude is even more striking. There can be no doubt that he introduces this character into *Die Soldaten* in the first place in order to pay tribute to the benevolence and sensitivity of the real-life Gräfin. Yet even here he also ends up emphasizing the gap between her selfless, committed concern and her impotence as an agent. Like Eisenhardt (Lenz shows) she is unable to understand the remorseless social pressures at work in the situation which she tries to remedy. All along the Gräfin sees Marie's predicament as stemming from a profound romantic infatuation. In order to extricate herself Marie has only to attach her yearning to someone in her own social sphere:

> Ihr einziger Fehler war, daß Sie die Welt nicht kannten, daß Sie den Unterschied nicht kannten, der unter den verschiedenen Ständen herrscht, daß Sie die Pamela gelesen haben, das gefährlichste Buch, das eine Person aus Ihrem Stande lesen kann. (225)

Lenz shows that this represents a complete misunderstanding; Marie's head has not been turned by reading romantic literature, and in a real sense she knows the world and the gulf between the classes only too well. But the Gräfin remains strangely blind. Even the fact that Marie, once she thinks she has lost Desportes, should turn her affections first to the Gräfin's own son and then to Desportes' fellow-officer, Mary, does not open her eyes to the fact that the driving force behind her passion is not really an erotic attachment to one individual but a compulsive social ambition which cuts her off for good from her middle-class background. Here again, as in the case of the Geheimrat and Eisenhardt, the aristocratic individual, for all his concern, is unable to guage the sheer force of the environmental pressures impinging upon the driven middle-class character and for this reason remains divorced from the real heart of his dilemma.

The portrayal of the *raisonneur* focuses, it seems to me, a deep unresolved tension which pervades all Lenz's plays. However seriously he takes the genuine idealistic concern of these figures, he still tends, consciously or unconsciously, to discredit and devalue it by highlighting its ultimate ineffectiveness. This probing, exposing energy is the real shaping impetus of his creative imagination. This always functions most powerfully when it is laying bare: when it reveals inner division and delusion beneath the facade of stable personality and probes impotence and anxiety at the heart of ordinary day-to-day relationships. The great innovative achievement of Lenz as a playwright lies in his exploration of the tormented life of the helpless, distraught individual in an alien, seemingly futile world. His search for a reformed and regenerated society was constantly offset by an overwhelming feeling of horror. To be a writer of comedies, as he suggests in *Pandamonium Germanicum*, was to live with this horror:

Ach ich nahm mir vor hinabzugehn und ein Maler der menschlichen Gesellschaft zu werden: aber wer mag da malen wenn lauter solche Fratzengesichter unten anzutreffen. (260)

Chapter 4

THE DEVELOPMENT OF DOMESTIC TRAGEDY:
MERCIER, GOETHE, WAGNER

I

Domestic drama as it developed in the 1760's was an intimate, essentially 'private' mode which sought to assert the priority of the world of home and family over the impersonal world of society and the state.[1] Underlying all the main theoretical discussions of the new form from Diderot to Lessing was the conviction that the narrow, close-knit realm of the family is the real arena of the individual's moral existence: that here in his intimate relationships and day-to-day responsibilities he confronts his most profound experiences and effectively shapes his destiny.

This domestic or 'bürgerlich' drama did not, as its advocates saw it, represent the outlook or interests of one social group; on the contrary, its aim was to express that most fundamental area of emotional and moral experience which was common to all men and which underlay all specific social-cultural distinctions.[2] It thus did not in their view represent any reduction or division of the great traditional concerns of the drama but rather an attempt to penetrate to the most profound, unchanging levels of human awareness.

This view of the primacy of the familial world was rooted in the conviction that the man who was caught up in the wider sphere of public, political activities was trapped in circumstances which in some way overlaid or distorted his essential humanity. The 'public' man was driven by fears and ambitions which were extraneous and which in their hold over him cut him off from those fundamental modes of experience which all men have in common. This did not mean, however, as these theorists insisted, that kings, rulers and generals were barred from the new 'middle-class' drama; its aim was precisely to go beyond the accidental, estranging pressures of such public status and lay bare the essential selfhood which bound them to all other human beings.[3] Diderot, for instance, made this quite clear in his *Entretiens sur le fils naturel*:

Si la mère d'Iphigénie se montrait un moment reine d'Argos et femme du
général des Grecs, elle ne me paraîtrait que la dernière des créatures. La
véritable dignité, celle qui me frappe, que me reserve, c'est le tableau de
l'amour maternel dans toute sa vérité.[4]

In the *Hamburgische Dramaturgie* Lessing made the same point
even more forcibly:

Die Namen von Fürsten und Helden können einem Stücke Pomp und Maje-
stät geben; aber zur Rührung tragen sie nichts bei. Das Unglück derjenigen,
deren Umstände den unsrigen am nächsten kommen, muß natürlicherweise
am tiefsten in unsere Seele dringen; und wenn wir mit Königen Mitleiden
haben, so haben wir es mit ihnen als mit Menschen, und nichts als mit Königen. Macht ihr Stand schon öfters ihre Unfälle wichtiger, so macht er sie
darum nicht interessanter. (76)

All the advocates of the new 'bürgerlich' drama in the 1760's
saw it as a mode dedicated to the presentation of what Valdrasti
termed 'die gemeinschaftliche Menschennatur' – of those most
basic emotional and moral impulses which govern the inward life of
the self beyond the reach of the random world of society.[5] If we
look closely at the discussions of the drama in this decade we can
see that the belief in the central moral significance of the private,
familial world was closely bound up with the assumption that this
world is essentially orderly and morally coherent. With its inescapable demands and binding obligations it represents, critics constantly
presumed, a clearly defined and unified arena in which the individual conducts his life in close interaction with those around him. It
is above all a personal world fully responsive to the aims and decisions of responsible moral agents. Only Lessing develops in any
detail a view of the drama as a form which expresses the wholeness
and integrity of a coherent moral world, but similar assumptions
clearly underlie the discussions of Diderot and the other advocates
of the new drama.[6] They all proceed from the belief that the realm
of the family is in a real sense outside, and exempt from, the incalculable forces of the public-political sphere. Consciously or unconsciously these theorists of domestic drama are intent on defining a
mode which is accountable and self-contained, which reflects an
ethical universe beyound the reach of the contingent circumstances
of historical actuality.[7]

II

Mercier, as we have seen, seeks to define a new form of domestic drama, which overcomes the limitations of this narrowly 'private' mode and reflects the wider processes of social existence as a whole. He sees the *drame* as upholding the psychological depth and moral force of the work of Diderot while significantly extending the scope of its main preoccupations. Its final purpose is, however, still affirmative and reconciliatory. It explores the involvement of the family in the tensions of contemporary society but aims in the end to show that at its deepest level society depends upon, and is responsive to, the seminal values embodied in the world of close interpersonal contact.

Mercier made a concerted attempt to realise his conception of the *drame* in a series of popular, theatrically effective plays from 1769 onwards. If we look at these works in the context of his theatrical aims, however, we are struck by the very narrow range of the playwright's effective concerns. Although he attaches great importance to the socially illuminating possibilities of the *drame* in his discussions, Mercier in practice constantly restricts the conflict in his plays to a very confined sphere of domestic relationships. The characters, it is true, do frequently speak of society and decry its evils, but the developments which form the action of the play take place in the world of the family. It is here in these close relationships, Mercier is insisting, and not in the wider anonymous world beyond, that oppression and exploitation come into being, and since they arise in this sphere they are necessarily subject to the control of responsible individuals.

The objects of Mercier's critical scrutiny in all these works are thus explicitly limited.[8] For instance, in *La Brouette du Vinaigrier* (1775) and in the later work *Zoë*, in which he examines tensions within the family circle, he makes it quite clear that he is not questioning its authoritarian structure as such. He does not query the traditional right of the father to control the household or even to arrange the marriages of his children (140 f.; 161; 210). What he is denouncing is rather the unfeeling pride and self-will of particular fathers which cloud their judgement and make them incapable of using their authority wisely and in the long-term interests of their children.

The character of Mercier's didactic purpose here is essentially conservative. He aims to show the disastrous effects of the misuse of paternal power in order to summon fathers everywhere to reassess a responsibility which is sacred, indeed God-given, and which society and the individual must therefore treat with the utmost respect.

Similarly, in *Le Faux Ami*, in which the dramatist explores the deepening estrangement between husband and wife, he makes it clear that he is not criticizing marriage as an institution but rather the attitudes and conduct of the partners which threaten the basis of their marriage (111, 181). It is egotism and a lack of self-knowledge, he shows, which have prevented them from living up to the obligations which their married state imposes on them. Misunderstanding and conflict arise out of personal moral failures for which husband and wife and other treacherous individuals outside the home must bear full responsibility.

Once again the impetus of Mercier's critical purpose is to vindicate the existing institutional structure of society. He insists explicitly that marriage is both the only basis on which an ultimately fulfilling relationship between man and woman can develop and at the same time the only foundation on which a stable, ordered society can grow and flower (190 ff.).

The restricted scope of Mercier's critical concern is even more striking in two plays, *L'Indigent* and *Le Juge*, in which he observes the working of the law. In neither work does he criticize the legal process as such or even the character of any individual law. He is denouncing rather the way the law is misused, deliberately and consistently, by cynical self-seeking men intent on exploiting and suppressing those who are dependent upon them. In *Le Juge*, for example, Mercier soon makes clear that he is not questioning the laws controlling the relations between landlord and tenant. The fact that the landlord abuses his power over his poor and uneducated tenants does not reveal a failure in the legal structure, but a fundamental lack of humanity in this one rapacious individual for which he alone is responsible and for which he can be called to account (31 f.; 56). Conversely, the dramatist shows that Leurye is a just, socially beneficent judge not primarily because of his professional skill but because he brings to the exercise of his work those qualities of sensitivity, honour, and moral concern which characterize his private existence. He is a good judge because he is a good man; his ability to overcome conflict and disorder in the community reflects the depth of his inherent compassion and humanity (61 f.; 94 f.; 97).

In these and his other plays written in this period Mercier's concern is to show that the evils which blight the life of society stem from the aggressive, wilful self-interest of individual men. These are not the helpless vessels of an oppressive system but responsible agents who chose to put their own advantage before what they know to be their inescapable obligations. And since they do bear this knowledge in themselves, they are always − the dramatist insists − capable of moral renewal. These plays all enact a decisive process of inner disruption and change. The action in each case culminates in a situation in which the self-seeking, exploitative individual is forced to face the implications of his behaviour. The dramatic climax takes the form of a self-encounter in which the latent moral energies in the protagonist break through the deadening hold of habituated egotism and prejudice and enable him to see his life in a new perspective.

Mercier puts forward this spectacle of inner renewal in the form of a direct summons to the spectator − a summons to grasp his existence as part of the sustaining process of corporate life and thus as bound by the great fundamental obligations (and possibilities) which this involves.

We have seen that in his theoretical writings Mercier defines the *drame* as a wide-ranging, realistic form capable of giving a strong, involving image of social actuality. When we turn to the plays themselves, it is very noticeable, however, that the action develops within a very narrow sphere of interpersonal encounter and that the wider world of society, though often rhetorically invoked, remains beyond the reach of his real imaginative concern. This is certainly in keeping with his didactic purpose which is to show that the evils of society stem from the immoral and insensitive actions of single men. Individual agents − he insists over and over again − are the cause of social injustice and tension, and at the same time the means by which they can be overcome.

There is just one work, *Le Deserteur*, written in 1770, in which Mercier seems to go beyond this fixed and limiting conception. Here he does present the dramatic figures as the victims of socially ratified forces and institutions which they morally reject but over which they have no control.

In this play Mercier denounces the prevailing code of military discipline as unjust, inhumane and devoid of all higher moral sanction. This code, it is true, seeks to derive an ostensible justification from the belief of rulers that is necessary to strip men of their humanity in order to turn them into lethal instruments of destruction. But this belief, Mercier shows, is itself unfounded, because it has no valid moral purpose in the modern world. What is it, the war-beleaguered people reflect, but the sport of kings, who make men's lives the pawns in an appalling game?

The dramatist does not pursue the political implications of this rhetorical denunciation, however, but concentrates on the narrower question of how military discipline actually operates and how it impinges on the lives of ordinary men. His purpose is to show that it is barbaric and evil because it ignores the frailties of men crushed and demoralized by the nightmare brutalities of war. 'La loi homicide' is blind, mechanical and unforgiving.

The action of the play demonstrates this institutionalized inhumanity. It shows the revolt and defection of a young soldier, Durimel, who is driven into a bemused hopelessness by his experience of war. The law makes no allowance for this despair which disturbs the stability of the young man's mind and suspends his normal capacities of thought. It can only brand him as a deserter and pronounce an automatic death-sentence (142 f.).

The supreme crisis in Durimel's life comes after his defection, when as a hunted man he comes face to face with his father, St. Franc, who is still a loyal serving officer. For now it is no longer a question of whether he can make good his escape but of reconciling his quest for freedom with the demands of family respect and responsibility (184 ff.). Soon Durimel is forced to see that only his death can resolve this contradiction. He recognizes that love for his father involves honouring his oath of allegiance which he still holds sacred, respecting the moral integrity which gives life and purpose to the older man. Thus when St. Franc, who has been given charge of his son, urges him to flee before it is too late, Durimel refuses (218 ff.). He resolves to accept death at the hands of the firing-squad rather than compromise the honour of the father, whom he loves above all. Out of love Durimel, in other words, voluntarily gives his life to a system he knows to be unjust and inhumane. At the moment of irrevocable choice he is impelled by an unquestioning sense of personal obligation towards his father which eclipses all general social-ethical considerations.

The dramatic action which begins with the denunciation of the futility of war and the senseless cruelty of the ways in which it is pursued, issues in a positive, reconciliatory climax – a climax which aims to assure the spectator of the value of his existence in a moral universe. For the sacrificial death of the hero, as Mercier presents it, reveals man's ability to perceive and respond to an ultimate, religious order of being which transcends all the relative contradictions of actual existence in society. It celebrates the moral heroism of Durimel and in so doing contrives to banish the unresolved evils of military life which society still accepts, from the consciousness of the spectator.

Le Deserteur shows in a particularly extreme form the tensions which pervade all Mercier's attempts to put forward a programme of social criticism within a framework of ultimate metaphysical and moral affirmation. The conception of these plays is torn by conflicting concerns and modes of perception in a way which the dramatist was never able to resolve. They culminate, as we have seen, in a demonstration of the inner freedom and rationality of the dramatic agents. In order to assert this positive view of the characters Mercier locates the dramatic action in an intimate sphere of interpersonal relations which is almost completely insulated from the wider historical-social situation. Here in this narrow world he can show the power of the individual to choose and to act and through his actions to determine the character of the world in which he lives. This is certainly in keeping with Mercier's reformist aim and particularly with his desire to appeal directly to the conscience of the individual spectator, but it restricts his concern to make the *drame* a vehicle of social exploration and comment which plays such a large part in his theoretical considerations of the form. Indeed, it seems to me that his moral purpose intrudes to such an extent on his expository concerns that it brings about a noticeable split in the presentation of the dramatic figures.

In the early parts of the action in all these plays Mercier seems intent on portraying the characters as beings caught up in the pressures of a particular social milieu and subject to their constraint. This analytical view is never developed, however. In the course of the dramatic action it gives way more and more to a desire to reveal the autonomy of the characters – to present them as essentially self-sufficient centres of unconditioned moral activity. The problem is that, as far as I can see, there is no real continuity or interaction

81

between these two conflicting viewpoints. The insight into the relativising force of social influences which pervades the dramatic exposition simply gives way to the demonstration of the inner freedom of the characters which forms the climax of the plays – a demonstration which tends to detach the dramatic action from the sphere of concrete social conditions.

The force of Mercier's moral purpose thus contrives to undermine his quest for a new kind of synthesis. It thwarts that attempt to integrate empirical, artistic and ethical concerns in a new imaginative whole which Mercier regards as the essential purpose of the new form. This is most obvious in works like *L'Indigent* and *La Brouette du Vinaigrier* in which he seeks to extend the range of social observation in the drama. Mercier emphasizes the fact that the main figures here are poor, uneducated and socially oppressed and yet are nonetheless able to function as the protagonists of significant dramatic conflict. He is also clearly aware that this view marks a break with older conceptions of domestic drama. What is novel is precisely Mercier's concern to stress the poverty, insecurity and constricted outlook of such characters – to draw attention to their social situation as the determining condition of their lives. He seems in fact to be emphasizing their dependence, vulnerability as the key to understanding their outlook and behaviour. The dramatist does not, however, develop this apparently deterministic approach. It soon becomes clear indeed that his intention is quite the opposite. We see before long that he is showing the dependence and exposure of these characters only to emphasize in a stronger and more moving way the psychic resources which enable them to rise above all material constraints and acknowledge the moral imperatives within them. The empirical view of the characters trapped in adverse socio-economic circumstances is displaced by a concern to show their inborn spiritual energies which can be suppressed but not destroyed.

This contradiction pervades all Mercier's work. It is not possible to see it as stemming from his inability as a creative artist to realize an ambitious but coherent theory of a new kind of drama. This basic tension between empirical insight and moralistic concern is also inherent in his dramaturgical theories and is already clearly apparent in his preface to *Jenneval*, which is his first major discussion of his aims as a dramatist.

Both in his theoretical discussions and in his plays Mercier gives the impression of addressing new possibilities for the drama which he himself, given his narrow and compelling moral aims, cannot fulfil. He seems to suggest innovative views of motivation and dramatic action only to leave them unrealized. He takes, as it were, a step towards a radical dramatic realism, anticipates a new conception of the relationship between social actuality and dramatic form, yet creates works which remain deeply rooted in traditional moral assumptions and pursue highly conventional didactic ends.

III

Faust in ursprünglicher Gestalt or the *Urfaust* as it is now generally known, is the version of the play which Goethe took with him when he left Frankfurt for Weimar in November 1775. It is an incomplete but intensely wrought work which has a peculiar, although still strangely undefined place in the development of domestic drama in Germany.[9] This is no doubt due in part to the fact that the fragment is divided in itself and that only the second part, the so called 'Gretchentragödie', constitutes a domestic play in any recognized sense. The fragment represents in fact a powerfully experimental attempt to bring together, to counterpose, two different modes of tragedy, two conflicting kinds of tragic awareness.[10] Throughout Goethe emphasizes the fact that the main figures, Faust and Gretchen, inhabit separate spiritual worlds. Each, he shows, lives out an experience of tragic contradiction and despair which is inaccessible to the other. Their encounter ends in catastrophe but it is a catastrophe which each experiences alone, trapped in his isolation and helplessness. Goethe had already anticipated this perception of tragic estrangement in *Clavigo* but here he is out to develop it in a much more intense and abrasive way. Here, in contrast to *Clavigo*, he stresses the heroic, metaphysical and thus necessary character of the remorseless striving of the protagonist, while at the same time attributing to the heroine an ability to experience horror and desolation, which establishes her more and more clearly (in marked contrast to Marie) as a tragic agent in her own right.[11]

Faust appears from the beginning of the fragment as an individual who acknowledges with a sharp, defiant pride his tragically divided selfhood. He knows that his will to self-realisation can never be sated because it seeks to transcend the limits of finite human experience (369 ff.). At the same time he is equally conscious that his relentless striving is also at odds with a desire for acceptance and peace which is also rooted deep in his being. Even as he yearns for higher and higher kinds of fulfilment he is aware that this longing for self-limitation and repose can never be stilled (388 f.).

Goethe sets Faust's encounter with Gretchen in the context of this insoluble predicament. From the first Faust feels himself irresistibly drawn to the harmony and strength of her fixed and ordinary existence. In her tiny room he senses something for which he has been longing largely unawares:

> Wie atmet rings Gefühl der Stille,
> Der Ordnung, der Zufriedenheit!
> In dieser Armut welche Fülle!
> In diesem Kerker welche Seligkeit.

He yearns to lose himself in the innocence and emotional power which, as he senses, flow from her rootedness in the sustaining life of the community, and in which he feels the possibility of release from his inner torment. Yet even at the height of his desire to possess Gretchen he is never able completely to subdue an insidious sense of foreboding. Goaded by the malicious scorn of Mephistopheles he fights to suppress the realisation that his love for all its renewing force must one day fall prey to his relentless quest for ever greater self-realisation (399; 403). It is only after he has deserted Gretchen and seen her utter despair that he can clearly recognize what in some part of himself he has known all along: that their lives are in inescapable contradiction, that his love must destroy her (415).

Goethe presents Faust's love for Gretchen in the first place as a stage in his irresistible pursuit of supreme fulfilment. He thus sets it in an ironical perspective which forces us from the beginning to see its conditional, transitory character and to sense at once the terrible exposure of the girl who gives herself to him heart and soul. Gretchen, however, does not appear simply as the victim of Faust's titanic striving. As he engaged himself with this figure Goethe was clearly drawn more and more to explore her experience from within and to sense its compelling tragic intensity. In this experience he came to see (it would appear) a dereliction which was tragic both in its finality and in its shattering emotional force, and which was at the same time grounded in the everyday world of society in a quite new and challenging way.

Gretchen's suffering, as Goethe presents it, is essentially inward. None of the other characters can enter into it and she herself is unable to grasp it by conscious thought. Faust, it is true, does sense that her existence is so deeply enmeshed in the life of the community that she could not withstand any conflict with its rigid demands (400; 408 f.). This dependence, however, he seems to see in external terms as a subjection to the repressive authority of a narrow Church-dominated society. To some extent this is obviously true but Goethe shows that her anguish stems not so much from her isolation from the community as from a rending experience of self-estrangement which in the end overwhelms her. And this experience, as the dramatist makes clear, is inseparably bound up with the great emotional and sensual awakening she had undergone in her love for Faust. In her passionate commitment to him she seems suddenly to break through her narrow, socially constricted view of her own being and to see herself and her existence in a new way. She gives herself to Faust with an open, spontaneous joy which, although it contradicts the teaching of the Church, she affirms as the expression of all that is best in herself. Although she recognizes her sin, her final awareness is positive and defiant:

> Doch alles, was mich dazu trieb,
> Gott! war so gut! ach, war so lieb. (410)

Despite her intense and deeply conventional piety Gretchen in effect asserts her own unique experience of love against the dictates of her religious upbringing. Although she never ceases to see herself as a conforming member of the community, it is clear that she has at some vital level freed herself from the constraining force of her environment and has in fact achieved a degree of inner independence which she cannot acknowledge even to herself.

It is this passion, in all its consuming power, which is the root of Gretchen's despair. This does not flow simply from the realisation that Faust has deserted her, but more profoundly from the insidious force of self-hatred which this realisation precipitates. In her loneliness and terror she is pierced by the awareness that this love is not the source of joy and renewal (as she had felt) but of a deep and irreparable remorse. In the grip of this blind, reckless power she has made herself guilty as she now sees of her mother's death, of giving birth to a bastard child and thus of incurring the condemnation of the Church and of the whole community (412 f.).

Goethe lets us see that it is above all the terrible certainty that she has brought this horrifying sequence of events upon herself, that she is to blame, which in the end destroys her. The disabling intensity of this awareness of guilt seems to stem from its power to release all the suppressed dread and confusion which were latent from the first in her passionate surrender to Faust. Even at the time of her fiercest yearning there lurked beyond the edge of consciousness, as now becomes apparent, a superstitious horror of her sexual desire; even while she was affirming the triumphant happiness of her love she was struggling to repress the consciousness that she had sinned and must face a terrible retribution.

The presentation of the catastrophe in *Urfaust* is charged by a tension between the external developments (of which all the characters are aware) and the nightmare significance which these acquire in the primitive, terrorised mind of the helpless Gretchen. We can see that what to her is infallible proof of divine condemnation is in no sense a necessary consequence of her seduction. We are aware, for instance, that she is not responsible for her mother's death (as this is Mephistopheles' doing); we can also see that it is not any failure in her love which causes Faust to desert her. The fact that she is driven to see these and the other disasters which befall her as proof of her immense guilt appears rather as the symptom of a terrible helplessness – a bondage to the demands of an oppressive environment which penetrate to the very core of her affective life. We are able to see that the heightening spiral of self-disgust which in the end destroys her, stems from her dependence on notions of impurity and defilement which have governed her understanding of herself since birth and which distort her emotional responses in ways she cannot understand.

The blind, unreasoning urge to murder her bastard child appears as the shattering climax of this process of inner breakdown. It marks the final disintegration of a mind so warped by guilt and despair that it yearns only for extinction – the extinction not just of her bastard child but also of her own racked and violated being.

Goethe presents the catastrophe in *Urfaust* in a harshly dissonant perspective. He emphasizes the gap between the outer developments of the action and their impact on the anguished, breaking mind of the heroine in a way which forces us to work towards an understanding of her suffering not available to any of the dramatic characters. He drives us in particular to go behind Gretchen's metaphysical experience of judgement and condemnation and to see it as a consequence of her helpless exposure to the estranging force of social determinants which divide her against herself and thrust her into ever deepening confusion. In the suffering of the heroine the dramatist is showing the power of society to bind the individual and warp his most profound inborn impulses. In this respect his aim is very close to that of Lenz. But whereas for Lenz this bondage to impersonal circumstance negates the very possibility of significant tragic experience,[12] Goethe seeks to grasp it as the source of genuine tragic suffering. And this seems to me both new and prophetic. In the *Urfaust* the dramatist seems intent on confronting an awareness of the absoluteness of the inner world of the heroine, her capacity to experience ultimate despair and dereliction, with a reductive, analytical view of her dependence on contingent social forces. At the very heart of Goethe's tragic vision is the awareness that Gretchen, for all her longing and strength of passion, is prey to compulsions in herself which are imposed on her by her environment and which are so deeply assimilated into her being that she cannot see them for what they are.

Goethe's conception of the tragic development in the *Urfaust* grows out of the awareness of a basic contradiction between the inborn, vital humanity of the heroine and the overwhelming, oppressive power of her environment. His attempt to evoke the full pathos of her suffering is inseparably bound up with the will to indict the repressive, life-denying society which condemns her to self-estrangement and despair. The intensity of Goethe's imaginative involvement with the stricken Gretchen reveals a desire not just to question the relentless striving of Faust but also to reject the moral assumptions of a whole corrupt social order — an order which he summons his contemporaries to measure against their own.

There have been few incisive attempts to assess the place of Wagner's work in the development of domestic drama. Most critics have restricted their interest, perhaps not surprisingly, to *Die Kindermörderin*. But even this has often been further limited by their preoccupation with Goethe's claim that in this play Wagner plagiarized *Urfaust*. This limitation of interest is symptomatic of a wide-spread presumption, which still persists among critics, that Wagner's dramas lack genuine creative originality and can be most profitably approached from the point of view of their dependence on earlier works, whether these are by Lessing, Goethe or Mercier.[13] It is this presumption which more than anything else has distracted attention from the strong innovative impetus in Wagner's work and from his serious quest for a new kind of tragic realism. Commentators have too often criticized his dependence as a playwright on the crude, melodramatic methods of the popular theatre without acknowledging his attempts to inform these with a rigorous new meaning. If we are to gain a fuller understanding of Wagner's work, we must, I think, take seriously his deep intuitive sense of the peculiar social relevance of conventional theatrical forms: his sense that the antagonisms rending the contemporary world had all the strident compulsiveness and violence characteristic of the traditional world of melodrama.

In *Reue nach der Tat* (1775) Wagner explores the relationship between Langen, a prosperous, highly cultured member of the Viennese upper-middle class, and Fridericke the daughter of the imperial coachman. At the beginning of the action Langen is intent on marrying Fridericke but has not yet proposed to her because he wants first to gain the consent of his mother, the arrogant and snobbish Justizrätin who is vehemently opposed to his love for a girl so much his social inferior (482; 489 f.). Langen, however, clearly does not see his marriage as dependent on his mother's consent. Since the death of his father he has assumed all the responsibilities of the head of the household and he is aware that he is free, legally and economically, of his mother's authority (507 f.). After he has made a last unavailing attempt to win her round he decides to propose to Fridericke and announce their engagement as soon as possible (499 f.; 504 f.).

Langen's view of the situation reveals a serious misunderstanding of the feelings of the girl he claims to know and love. In expecting her to marry him against his mother's will he is demanding of her an independence of judgement and emotional response of which, as becomes more and more evident, she is simply not capable. She has been brought up in a very close-knit, affectionate family and accepts without question the absolute authority of her widowed father whom she adores. It is thus not surprising that she is unable to entertain the idea of a marriage which does not enjoy the blessing of both sets of parents (504 ff.). Even though she sees that the objections of the Justizrätin are rooted in vanity and prejudice she still feels in her heart that it is wrong to defy her. In fact, it soon becomes clear that she attributes a near-supernatural significance to the act of parental blessing itself, regarding it as a power which guarantees the wellbeing and good fortune of the married couple throughout their life together. Langen's suggestion that they should marry against his mother's will fills her with a deep sense of dread and apprehension which she finds hard to express and quite impossible to analyze.

Langen is deeply perplexed by the extremity of Fridericke's reaction but, as Wagner is at pains to show, he is himself by no means exempt from the same irrational impulses which beset her. Although he prides himself on his clear-sighted rationality and is quite convinced that he is morally in the right, he too is shaken by this conflict with his mother in ways which he cannot grasp. This is most obvious in his involuntary horror when he learns of the story of the stricken Jew who was cursed by his father for marrying against his will and was subsequently haunted by limitless misfortune and disaster (506 ff.). Langen's deepening consternation here betrays some lurking superstitious fear of parental anger and retribution which is utterly at odds with his view of himself as an enlightened, self-responsible individual.

Wagner's aim is to show that the opposition of the Justizrätin plunges both the lovers into a severe emotional crisis which neither can fully confront. This crisis seems to be at the centre of the dramatist's analytical preoccupation. He is concerned, it would appear, to explore in painstaking detail the conflict between the search of the two young people for a love which promises happiness and lasting fulfilment, and their exposure to deep irrational pressures which flow from their social experience. Midway through Act

89

IV, however, Wagner seems to break off his close psychological scrutiny and presents a series of extreme developments which alter the situation of the lovers for good. The Justizrätin brings a serious complaint about the behaviour of her son to the Empress who orders that Fridericke be detained in a convent and Langen prevented from seeing her until he renounces his determination to marry her (515; 519). It is clear that Wagner does not regard this intervention by the Empress as disrupting the coherent development of the dramatic action. He sees it rather as an accelerating factor — as heightening those fears and confusions which already possess the lovers to the point where they acquire irreversible force. Yet although the playwright makes repeated attempts to minimize the responsibility of the Empress, her intervention does seem to bring about a catastrophe which would not otherwise have taken place. For it is above all the violent, unexpected separating of the two lovers and all the fear and humiliation this involves which really brings about the final catastrophe. Langen collapses in nervous exhaustion while Fridericke is driven into a fit of despair so intense that she takes her own life (531 f.). The vanity and class-prejudice of the Justizrätin certainly sets this process of disruption in train but she cannot — as Wagner openly insists (532 ff.) — be held responsible for its devastating outcome. The dramatist does succeed in revealing the exposure of both Langen and Fridericke to strong subliminal pressures but he is not able to show these as having compelling, lethal force.

In *Reue nach der Tat* Wagner is taking a first tentative step towards an analytical domestic drama. The shaping forces of the action stem from contradictions in the characters which he exposes in close detail. At the same time, however, he still tries to show the unfolding of these inner contradictions by means of methods of intrigue taken over from the conventional theatre. The problem from the point of view of his intention lies in the fact that the crucial developments seem to come from an area beyond the relationship of the two lovers, to impinge upon this and alter it in an irreversible way. Although he effectively lays bare the tensions in their experience these do not appear in themselves to have the remorseless destructive power which he seeks to attribute to them. This basic weakness in *Reue nach der Tat* stems from Wagner's failure to grasp in vivid psychological detail the destructive divisions he senses in the consciousness of the two protagonists. Although his concep-

90

tion of the action is essentially analytical he fails to develop the discriminating empirical methods of presentation which were necessary to its effective dramatic realisation. This is most evident in his failure to grasp the pressures inherent in the day-to-day life of the two families with any penetrating force. It is noticeable that he is content merely to counterpose in a flatly conventional way the unity and emotional warmth in the household of the coachman with the arid, pretentious formality of the home dominated by the Justizrätin, but makes no attempt to analyze the environmental forces which shape the character of relationships in the two families. It is above all this bland, undiscriminated presentation of the familial life of the two lovers which thwarts Wagner's intention, since it deprives the tensions in their experience of that deeper social force he clearly ascribes to it. And this failure to evoke effectively the exposure of the two main figures in the everyday life of society makes them appear – in the face of Wagner's express intentions – the victims of the arbitrary power of the Court.

Die Kindermörderin is a much more ambitious and challenging work. Both in his perception of the exposure of the individual in the everyday world and in his attempt to realise this in a cohesive tragic action, Wagner is making a much more far-reaching attempt to achieve a kind of probing analytical realism which is quite new in German drama.[14] Here, once again, he explores the predicament of two young people bound to each other by a love which defies the remorseless, unwritten laws of class-separation. Wagner shows that this love represents for both partners an emotional commitment which transcends the determining force of their social experience. The feelings of Evchen Humbrecht, the butcher's daughter, for Gröningseck, the aristocratic officer, does certainly involve naive, awe-struck admiration but it has a spontaneity and depth which are completely personal. So powerful is her attachment to him that it seems to undermine the ingrained habits of modesty and restraint which have governed her whole life in her ascetic middle-class environment. In her very first contact with him, as she confesses quite openly, she experienced a strong sexual attraction which influenced her behaviour decisively at the time of temptation (576). In this, as in other aspects of her behaviour, Wagner is out to establish Evchen as a girl of great sensual and emotional vitality who, despite her very restrictive upbringing and conventionality, is capable of a deep and mature devotion to the man she loves. Even the realisation that she is pregnant, though it shocks and horrifies her, does not destroy her belief that she and Gröningseck will be married and achieve happiness together (578 f.).

For Gröningseck too, as the dramatist makes clear, love is a supreme commitment. He appears as a man who has lived his life in an upper-class milieu and who takes great pride in his power to shape his own existence. He repeatedly insists that his love for Evchen overrides all other considerations and that nothing be allowed to stand in the way of their happiness (560 f.). In his determination to marry Evchen he is prepared to incur his father's anger, cut himself off from his family and even resign his commission and thus break the bond of loyalty which holds together the officer-corps (569 f.). Gröningseck never doubts that he is right to put his love for Evchen above everything and is confident that he can lead a fulfilled, happy existence with her outside the upper-class world to which he belongs.

Wagner thus establishes both Evchen and Gröningseck as individuals capable of deep mutual devotion who are ready to challenge the forces of prejudice and resentment which threaten their relationship. At the same time, however, the dramatist is intent on showing the peculiar exposure of the lovers in their everyday existence — an exposure all the more ominous as they themselves are unable to see it clearly. Both of them are prey to pressures in themselves and in the world around them which their belief in the power of their love treacherously hides from their view. In the middle parts of the action (Acts II and IV) Wagner probes this vulnerability primarily by means of a close, searching analysis of the experience of Evchen. Despite her repeated expressions of trust in Gröningseck he shows that she is increasingly infected by an elusive force of melancholy which seems to drain her of vitality and hope (557 f.; 571 f.). This probably stems in part, it is true, from the physical changes brought about by her pregnancy and from the fear that these may betray her shameful secret. Wagner clearly suggests, however, that such specific, understandable anxieties are just the symptom of a deeper anguish which has its roots in a compulsive sense of guilt — a guilt she cannot fully focus much less confront and which threatens to corrode her whole emotional existence. She is possessed — like the abandoned Gretchen — by the apprehension of some unspeakable horror which she has brought on herself and can never escape (576 f.).

92

As the dramatic action develops it becomes clear that Evchen is trapped in a maiming cycle of self-torment which threatens to undermine the balance of her mind. Her devouring awareness of failure seems to release visions of punishment and disaster which only serve to further heighten her compulsive sense of self-abhorrence. It is probably this view of the breakdown of the heroine which Goethe saw as most obviously 'stolen' from the *Urfaust*. Certainly Wagner's tragic perception here is strikingly similar, and there can be little doubt that his imagination was indeed impelled at a profound level by his knowledge (however superficial this may have been) of Goethe's play. At the same time, however, we must recognize that Wagner presents this process of psychic disintegration in a rather different way and seeks to assimilate it to his own distinctive conception of tragic conflict. He goes much further than Goethe in detaching the inward collapse of the heroine from her outer situation. The decisive disruption in the mind of Evchen takes place at a time when she still believes her relationship to Gröningseck to be intact and when she still hopes to marry him. Indeed in *Die Kindermörderin* it is the breakdown in the mind of the heroine which is the source of the false conviction that she has been deserted by the man she loves. For, as the dramatist takes great pains to suggest, the letter forged by Hasenpoth, Gröningseck's closest friend, merely serves to precipitate an expectation already formed in her subconscious mind. The news that her lover has abandoned her is no surprise; it comes rather as the confirmation of something she knows deep in herself to be inescapable (579 f.). She never doubts for a moment the authority of this letter which contradicts all that she claims to believe about the man she loves, because she has all along been awaiting its arrival.

This belief that she has been deserted by Gröningseck precipitates the final stages in the inner collapse of Evchen. In panic she flees from the fury of her father and the vindictive judgement of the community so that she can have her baby by herself and far from her usual surroundings. But even this escape cannot prevent the remorseless process of self-condemnation. For even here she is pursued by the rumours from the city that her mother has died of grief and that by common consent she, Evchen, is the murderer (597 f.). This overwhelms her with the force of a supreme unanswerable condemnation: 'Meine Mutter! gestorben! und ich schuld daran!' Here too she cannot doubt the truth of what she hears because her conscience has already indicted her.

It is above all the recognition of this unthinkable guilt which drives her over the edge of insanity. Trapped in inner blackness she strikes back wildly at her tormentors in the only way within her power. Her blind, frenzied urge to kill her bastard child shows a fury of self-revulsion which is heightened still further by an impotent desire to destroy the man who so cruelly betrayed her and the world which conspired in this betrayal (600 f.).

At the same time as Wagner explores the inner violation of Evchen he is also laying bare the helplessness of Gröningseck who in his own way is equally ensnared and disabled by hostile forces in his environment. The dramatist's aim in fact is to show the final catastrophe as arising out of the interaction of the two conjoining predicaments of the lovers as they struggle to remain true to each other in the face of an alien, treacherous world. Wagner is concerned to show that Gröningseck for all his aristocratic power and self-confidence is, like Evchen, the victim of the social milieu to which he belongs. He is blind to the real depth of his dependence on the life of the officer-corps and the standards it imposes – a blindness which is crucially apparent in his tense, ambiguous relationship with Hasenpoth, his closest friend and colleague. For the latter is able to intervene in the situation in a way which Gröningseck does not anticipate, even though he does so in the name of the officer-corps and in a concern to assert values which Gröningseck himself also generally recognises. Wagner goes out of his way to stress this representative character of Hasenpoth's intervention. He makes it clear that Hasenpoth does not act out of personal malice but of a driving sense of group loyalty which is the deepest emotional impulse of his existence. This is most evident in the deliberation with which Wagner sets this 'correction' of Gröningseck in parallel to the punishment of von Salis, an officer who reported a colleague for cheating at cards and who thus, like Gröningseck, was guilty of breaking one of the most basic unwritten laws of the officers' code (565 ff.). Hasenpoth – as Wagner portrays it – is undertaking the same retributive action towards his friend as the officer-group had taken collectively towards the man who threatened the cohesion of their shared existence. In both cases this defensive corporate reaction is marked by a violence which takes the unsuspecting victim completely by surprise and leaves him helpless.

Central to Wagner's tragic conception is the awareness of a crucial link between the outward vulnerability of Gröningseck in the officer-milieu and the inner helplessness of Evchen before the ravages of her anguished middle-class conscience. He sees the two kinds of subjection not just as akin but as inseparably related in ways which none of the dramatic figures can perceive. The tragic structure of the play, as Wagner sees it, expresses these two interacting processes of social determination in one coherent dramatic development.

Wagner is here pursuing a conception of tragic form which is both original and complex, and it is scarcely surprising that he was not fully successful in realising it in dramatic terms. Critics of the play from Erich Schmidt to Dosenheimer have spent much time diagnosing what they see as the incoherence of the plot – an incoherence focused in the arbitrary intrusion of the figure of Hasenpoth into the development of the action.[15] Although such discussions sometimes reveal an insensitive blindness to Wagner's intentions they do, I think, point to a real failure on his part to bring his tragic perception to full dramatic life. Even if we can sense, for instance, the function which Hasenpoth is supposed to fulfil, the fact remains that Wagner has not been able to endow his behaviour with the vicarious significance which he clearly felt it possessed. But this, it seems to me, is only one aspect of Wagner's wider failure to realise the officer-milieu or indeed the experience of Gröningseck with any compelling imaginative force. It is this detached and perfunctory presentation of the officer and his entrapment which more than any failure in plotting is the source of that impression of incoherence which critics have repeatedly expressed. For Wagner's lack of real imaginative engagement with the predicament of Gröningseck has the effect of reducing or relegating a whole aspect of the tragic situation which in terms of Wagner's total conception is inseparable from and, in the end equivalent to, the predicament of the heroine. The apparent weakness in plotting really reflects, in other words, the extreme onesidedness of Wagner's effective imaginative preoccupation. It is only when he is exploring the experience of Evchen and its rootedness in her narrow middle-class world that his creative imagination catches fire and works with full consuming intensity. But the very power of this exploration has an unbalancing effect. It lends the figure of the heroine a centrality and tends thus to isolate it in a way which obscures his ambitious view of the tragic development as an interaction of far-reaching environmental processes that control the lives of all the dramatic characters and reveal the existence of a whole society.

This attempt to grasp corporate existence fully and directly shapes Wagner's conception of *Die Kindermörderin*. His aim is to achieve a new and more challenging kind of dramatic realism. This is apparent in his analytical view of the action of the play as an unfolding of the antagonisms governing contemporary society. It is just as evident, however, in his concern to particularize the setting of the work in a quite novel way. He is clearly at pains to evoke this distinctive milieu of Straßburg in the early 1770's by insistent references to local streets, inns and other landmarks, and to well-known local events and individuals as well as by the (albeit very limited) use of Straßburg dialect.[16] This is characteristic of his sustained quest for a richer and more discriminated illusion of social actuality. Wagner makes considerable efforts to create a more vivid and authentic picture of the contrasting aristocratic and middle-class milieux than any of his contemporaries. At the same time he introduces settings – like the brothel (537 ff.) and the washer-woman's hut (593 f.) – which extend the social range of the drama of his time. More significant than all this, however, is the fact that Wagner is concerned to build these single images of corporate life into an integrated and, by contemporary standards, comprehensive picture of contemporary society. By means of protracted discussions and anecdotes (eg. pp. 550 ff.; 554 f.; 566 f.; 586) he constantly makes us aware of social conditions which lie beyond the scope of the immediate action but which are in fact intimately related to it. Wagner's ambitious aim is to show the shattered love of Evchen and Gröningseck as the symptom of a pervasive disorder in the life of a whole society – a disorder reflected in the bitterly conflicting attitudes to religion, morality, education, the law in the different social groups, as also, in a different way, in the prevalence of crime, begging, prostitution and the horrifying brutality of law-enforcement.

The tragic action, as Wagner saw it, was to appear as the intense shattering expression of a dissolute society torn by injustice and oppression and lacking all vitalising sense of corporate loyalty and purpose. All its pervading depravity and violence were (in his conception) gathered up, focused, in the subjection of the lovers and above all in the insanity of Evchen. The final outcome of the action, however, remains uncertain. Although the Fiskal explains that Evchen, like every other mother in recent years found guilty of killing her child, faces certain execution, the play ends with Gröningseck setting off for Versailles to beg the King for clemency.

The openess of this ending is deliberatley provocative. Wagner's purpose is to disconcert and challenge the contemporary spectator in a way which forces him to confront the actual circumstances of the world around him. We can see here now deeply his propagandist aim informs and directs his quest for heightened social authenticity. In attempting to create a compelling image of day-to-day life in contemporary Straßburg he is intent on breaking down the self-sufficiency of theatrical illusion – on destroying those barriers which were traditionally held to separate the spectator's experience of tragic suffering and his awareness of conflict and violation in the life of society around him.

V

Mercier, Goethe and Wagner all take over the form of the domestic drama and attempt in their different ways to make it an instrument of social exploration and criticism. Mercier sees the *drame* as superceding the 'private' family drama of the Enlightenment. Its function is to show the vulnerability of the individual in the contemporary world and to expose the forces of injustice and oppression. But although this conception is novel and potentially far-reaching Mercier's purpose is in the end profoundly conservative. He aims to show the responsibility and freedom of the dramatic characters: to vindicate their ability to direct their existence in the narrow everyday world in which they live. His plays thus have the effect of re-asserting the close-knit familial sphere as the decisive arena of the individual's destiny and in so doing of insulating this sphere (in a way which clearly contradicts all his intentions) against the processes which shape the life of society as a whole.

Goethe and Wagner, it seems to me, fulfil the radical impetus inherent in Mercier's view of the *drame*. Both seek to grasp the emotional-spiritual dependence of the individual in an alien, oppressive world as a form of subjection which in its relentless inevitability is inherently tragic. From the point of view of classicist theories of tragedy this concern to present the suffering of Gretchen or Evchen as tragic is essentially self-contradictory for it involves an attempt to relate a vision of ultimate metaphysical despair to a view of the determining power of social forces which are by their very nature contingent and changeable. In *Urfaust* and in Wagner's two tragedies the playwright's concern to draw the spectator imaginatively into the anguish of the heroine goes hand in hand with a desire to explore those destructive tendencies in corporate existence which divide her and estrange her from herself. Even as he forces us to respond to the inevitability of the process of inner breakdown he is intent on showing the arbitrary character of the circumstances which bring it about. While evoking the momentousness of the heroine's experience of despair the dramatist is laying bare those distorting pressures in her environment in a way which forces the spectator or reader to condemn them and thus, implicitly, to envisage (or, in Wagner's case, explicitly to work towards) their eventual removal.

The fragmented, ambivalent conception of tragedy expressed in these plays marks in my view a break-through of considerable historical importance. The attempt to see the individual both as the object and as the protagonist of the tragic process anticipates in a fundamental way, the search for new tragic possibilities in the drama of the 19th century. Here, in these probing, often uncertain, works we can recognise that will to assimilate inherited modes of tragic feeling to a rigidly empirical view of life, to make realistic awareness responsive to searching tragic suggestion, which impels the quest for new forms of realistic tragedy from Büchner to Hauptmann. This is something to which we will have to return.

Chapter 5

THE EARLY PLAYS OF F. M. KLINGER

I

No works of the Sturm und Drang have so divided critical opinion as the early plays of Klinger. Even among his friends and acquaintances they provoked violently conflicting responses, and ever
since attempts to assess his aims and achievements as a playwright
have differed just as irreconcilably.[1] No critic to my knowledge has
ever doubted that an understanding of Klinger's plays was essential
to a valid estimate of the drama of the Sturm und Drang as a
whole, yet every major trend in interpretation seems to have succeeded in precipitating an equally powerful counter-view. This is
very evident in the attempts to assess his work in the past sixty
years or so, when for the first time critics seemed to establish a
cohesive, increasingly discriminated view of Klinger's work. In the
1920's Korff and May pioneered a new understanding of Klinger's
plays as a powerful, imaginative expression of a radical individualism which voiced in an intense and highly personal way the driving
impulses of the whole epoch.[2] In the following decades commentators like Schneider and Newald succeeded in extending this basic
understanding of Klinger as the Sturm und Drang dramatist *par ex-
cellence* and establishing it as a generally accepted view which dominated criticism well into the post-war era.[3] The appearance of
Christoph Hering's book *Der Weltmann als Dichter* in 1966 marked
the beginning of a fundamental impetus towards critical re-assessment. By means of a closer, more imaginative study of biographical
sources combined with penetrating literary-critical analyses Hering
succeeded in challenging the received view of Klinger's involvement
in the Sturm und Drang. The dramatist – he claimed – belonged to
the movement only fleetingly, for certain periods during the time
between 1774-76, and even then only in a hesitant, ambivalent
way.[4] Pursuing this seminal conviction he went on to question the
deep-set presumption that Klinger the dramatist identifies himself
wholly with the heroic protagonists in his plays: that he proclaims

and affirms their titanic individualism with passionate, imaginative commitment. On the contrary, Hering insisted, the conception of these plays grows out of Klinger's awareness of deep unresolved inner tensions. He uses the dramatic form, in fact, as a means of exploring contradictions in his own make-up which, as he is all too aware, threaten the very foundations of his selfhood.[5] Far from celebrating the blind, assertive fury of his heroes, Klinger (in Hering's view) is seeking to distance himself from racking compulsions in himself, to find release from their irrational hold over his will and imagination.

This new critical approach has undoubtedly proved very fruitful. Hering's view of the essentially therapeutic character of Klinger's early plays has influenced almost all recent critical studies and is particularly evident in the attempts of commentators like Snapper, Guthke and Huyssen to re-assess the work of the dramatist in its relations to the Sturm und Drang.[6] There can be no doubt in my view that recent criticism has succeeded in bringing to light aspects of Klinger's plays which had gone largely unnoticed and in so doing has opened up quite new interpretative possibilities. At the same time, however, it seems to me just as clear that studies in the past few years have equally disregarded the findings of earlier critics which were valuable in their own terms and also afforded a tenable, cohesive understanding of Klinger's early work.

Although they are so deeply at odds, these two critical approaches seem able to co-exist without really impinging on one another. This would appear to point to some deep-lying ambiguity in the conception of these plays which, as far as I can see, critics have not yet fully explored.

It seems to me that any effort to re-assess Klinger's early work must begin with an attempt to penetrate the conflicting impulses which pervade his sense of the tragic — his distinctive vision of the power and vulnerability of his heroic figures.

II

Klinger's first two plays *Otto* (1775) and *Das leidende Weib* (1775) are tentative, experimental works in which he struggles to integrate his own distinctive tragic awareness with an essentially conventional sense of dramatic form. The tension between these two impulses is particularly evident in *Otto*. Here his concern to present a vivid stage-action, clearly modelled on Goethe's *Götz*, is strikingly at odds with his attempt to explore the tragic anguish of his lonely, brooding and largely inactive hero.[7] As the action of the play develops it soon becomes clear that all the complex intriguing of Bishop Adelbert and his henchman Graf Norman has no intrinsic tragic significance but is solely the mechanism by which the dramatist brings about the tragic crisis. All these machinations which make up so much of the external action serve merely to isolate Otto from Prinz Karl whom he loves with a consuming selfless devotion, and to thrust him into shattering emotional confusion (47 ff.; 87).

It is the utter vulnerability of Otto which is at the centre of Klinger's imaginative concern. He is totally helpless not just before the treachery of those who deceive and manipulate him, but also before the horrifying lust for revenge which overwhelms him when he believes himself betrayed (62). His impelling will to love which is the source of his passionate heroic power also represents a terrible exposure. For when this will is thwarted he is swept by a blind frenzy of hatred which perverts his deepest affective energies and estranges him irrevocably from himself:

Brich los, Zorn! Wuth! aller verderbender grimmiger Zorn, der je im Menschen war, ihn zu Mord und Greuel antrieb, haufe, wüthe in mir! Verblend meine Augen! Mein Hirn will ich ausschlagen, kommt mir ein andrer Gedanke als Blut, blutige Rache und Mord. Und, habe volle genügende Rache, so drück mirs Herz ab! geschandet will ich nicht leben. (102)

Klinger does not present this tragic predicament as a progressive inner conflict but rather as a state of possession – of the bondage of the self to alien impersonal forces which seem to invade it from without. The dramatist makes clear that the hero as a thinking, willing agent cannot impinge upon this inward state but must rather confront it passively as observer and interpreter (66).

This recognition of the inescapable contradiction within himself sets Otto apart from all the other dramatic figures. It isolates him both from those who betray and exploit him (42 ff.), and from Karl and his sister, Gisella, who claim to love and unterstand him (79 f.). Klinger indeed sees this irrevocable tragic anguish as raising the hero above the whole world of contingent circumstances and partial,

101

compromised relationships. He alone is aware of the irreconcilability of this contradiction which flows from the deepest impulse of his being. Klinger is at pains to set the experience of the hero against all the colliding aims and ambitions which determine his environment. These appear as the expression of an arbitrary, superficial quest for power which serves merely to emphasize the depth and finality of Otto's experience of violation. There is in Klinger's tragic conception no ironic impulse, no attempt to question the hero's experience or place it in a context which could relativize its imaginative impact or significance. The main thrust of his apprehension is to involve us fully in Otto's awareness of victimisation and self-loss which he knows to be irredeemable because it is rooted in his deepest creative potentiality. The dramatist seeks to draw us to identify ourselves as fully and intensely as possible with the racked hero who in his frenzied lust for revenge on the man he had loved, knowingly and irresistibly destroys himself.

In *Das leidende Weib* (1775) Klinger again attempts to adapt an established dramatic mode to his own novel tragic perception.[8] He takes over the form of domestic tragedy, but uses it in a way which seems directly to challenge contemporary developments in the genre. For unlike Wagner, for instance, he is not out to analyze a tragic predicament rooted in environmental processes. Klinger is certainly concerned to expose specific social evils such as the egotism and treachery of the court (24) or the self-indulgent hypocrisy of the young aesthetes (11 ff.), but these do not impinge upon the central tragic action. These revelations of social corruption serve solely as a contrast or foil — they highlight the consuming, selfless intensity of the love which binds Malchen, the wife of the Gesandte, and Brand, her childhood lover. They emphasize the gulf which separates this love from a degenerate, conniving world.

The dramatist makes it clear that Malchen's love for Brand is the impelling energy of her whole emotional life. It has dominated her awareness of herself and her existence since childhood, and even after her marriage it continues to obsess her, however hard she tries to suppress it (21 f.). Her emotional commitment to Brand is total; it is insusceptible to external pressures and beyond the control of her own conscious will. There is no flaw or tension in this love; her suffering arises solely from the fact that it is denied — that her father has chosen to disregard it and arrange for her to marry another man (28). It is this marriage which thrusts Malchen into a state of

102

fatal self-contradiction. For marriage to her – however it has been brought about – is sacred. It represents a vow taken before God which she regards as binding her absolutely (28 f.). Malchen is unable even for an instant to disregard the finality of her obligation to her husband and children.

At the same time, however, it is equally clear that her ethical conviction, however deep and impelling, cannot touch her passionate yearning for Brand. She is trapped in an inner conflict which, as she is more and more aware, she cannot resolve. It is this subjective experience of discrepancy which governs the dramatist's vital interest. He is concerned throughout to penetrate its hidden, inward significance, to probe the ways in which it pierces and lacerates her tormented mind. Malchen, Klinger shows, is never at peace. Even at moments of intense, passionate surrender she is haunted by a horrifying awareness of sin; in the very act of begging God's forgiveness she longs for the sin she repents. When Brand asks her why she is weeping she replies:

> Über meine Sünde, Brand! Und in meiner Brust brennt's – o fühl's, ich bin bereit, neue zu begehen. (27; cf. 17)

Every moment of her life she spends in a condition of maiming inner division. She begs her lover:

> Nun, so gib mir nur ein bißchen Ruhe, nur ein bißchen Ruhe; daß es mich nicht aufschrecke neben meinem Mann. Tu's um unsrer Liebe willen; nur ein bißchen Ruh' macht mich glücklich. (28)

As in *Otto* Klinger's aim is to draw us into this experience, to make us see it from within, as it were, through the eyes of the heroine. He wants us to feel the sheer compelling force of her love while at the same time sensing the full depth of her religious awareness of herself and her life before God. There is, as far as I can see, no explicative, analytical impulse in Klinger's apprehension of the heroine's predicament. Basic to his tragic conception is rather the awareness that this predicament is both inescapable and finally mysterious since its roots lie in her intrinsic make-up as an individual. Unlike Wagner in *Die Kindermörderin*, for instance, who is out to expose the determinateness of the heroine's moral awareness,[9] Klinger sees Malchen's conscience, like her love, as valid in its own right, as an organ of genuine spiritual meaning.

103

We can see here once again Klinger's tendency to see the tragic crisis as essentially separate from, and alien to, the working of environmental processes. This tendency is most evident, however, in the way he apprehends the crucial presupposition of the tragic action: the decision of Malchen's father to override her devotion to Brand and arrange her marriage to a man she cannot love. It is noticeable that we learn next to nothing about this decision — neither the circumstances in which it comes about nor the aims which impel it. Nor does Klinger relate it to the general outlook or philosophy of the Geheimrat.[10] In fact, it is very hard to see this decision as in keeping with his general behaviour in the dramatic present. Here he appears as a consistently caring and sensitive father who is genuinely concerned for his children's welfare and prepared to assert his own judgement in the face of convention (24). What makes this decision seem still more puzzling is the fact that the Geheimrat is even now, years later, clearly still well disposed towards Brand whom he treats as a valued friend of the family and tries to help professionally whenever he can (25). But the most striking aspect of Klinger's presentation is that he does not show any of the figures as reflecting seriously on this crucial decision. The Geheimrat betrays no misgivings about the way he has exercised his paternal authority, and the lovers themselves do not seem ever to have questioned or rebelled against this decision which has destroyed their whole world at a stroke. They, like the other characters, accept it as something irrevocable, something that has happened in the past which makes the present inescapably what it is.

Klinger's intention is obviously to distance this decisive action of the Geheimrat from which everything follows, to leave it essentially undefined. He does not explore the motives out of which it arises or the ways in which it impinges on the minds of the individual characters. He is intent on detaching it from any coherent process of motivation and thus, it would seem, on stylising it, lending it a wider suggestive force. His aim is perhaps to grasp it as a symbol of antagonism — of some force in life which negates man's deepest creative impulses and holds him in a state of self-alienating contradiction.

But however we interpret Klinger's strangely unrealised presentation of the Geheimrat's action, it is quite clear that it shapes Malchen's destiny irresistibly. Once her father has taken this step, she is condemned to an existence in which she is always at odds with herself, consumed at once by guilt and unfulfilled desire. Klinger sees the death of his heroine as the final break-down of her mind and body under the sheer force of this insoluble contradiction.

In *Das leidende Weib* — as in *Otto* — Klinger does not fully succeed in integrating his tragic perception with his sense of dramatic form. The great technical difficulty he faced stemmed from the fact that he saw the tragic contradiction in both works as a state of inner division which, since it is essentially fixed and unresolvable, he could not present as an unfolding process of conflict. The most intensely realised parts of both works are introspective passages in which the protagonist voices directly his awareness of agonising inner discrepancy.[11] It is noticeable, however, that these evocative tragic reflections remain largely separate from the external action. This lyrical apprehension of tragic predicament is also noticeably at odds with the realistic, analytical tendency which controls some parts of his dramatic presentation. Both in *Otto* and in *Das leidende Weib* he takes considerable pains to set the dramatic developments in a particularised social environment which encloses the whole action. Yet, as I have tried to show, what engages his creative imagination most profoundly is a perception of tragic violation which transcends the working of contingent empirical forces.

III

Klinger clearly learnt a great deal from confronting the problems which beset him in writing these two early plays. In his next work, *Die Zwillinge* (1776), which from the first was regarded as his most significant artistic achievement, he made a strong, innovative attempt to create a new kind of dramatic form — a form wholly informed by his vision of tragic victimisation. Here he did in fact succeed in realising an intense quality of dramatic integration in which outer event and inward reflection are fused in a powerful, sustained exploration of the tragically divided self.

The structure of *Die Zwillinge* is intensely analytical. The action, as Otto Ludwig noted, is in a real sense over before the play begins; the catastrophe is there palpably present in the opening words of the exposition.[12] Ludwig is here responding to the thrust of Klinger's concern to show the dramatic present as the issue of a remorselessly controlling past, and to grasp the whole life of the hero, Guelso, as a process of rending torment which is already complete and merely awaits its final outward consummation. Through the hero's raging memories and thoughts Klinger evokes a force of hatred which has devoured his whole life and now explodes in one climactic act of vengeance. In the very first scenes of the play it becomes clear that all Guelso's fury flows from a supreme childhood experience of betrayal (68 ff.). His whole sense of himself and his existence is charged with the outraged awareness that even in his cradle he was rejected by his mother and father who gave all their love to his twin brother, Ferdinando:

> Der Junge wird gekost, geleckt, geliebt, von Vater und Mutter, und ich steh' allenthalben in der Rechnung ein garstiges Nichts ... Mein Blut wird heiß, mein Zorn drängt sich hervor. (72)

Already he challenges his brother in his imagination:

> Ha dann, Heuchler! ich will dich lehren! Herausgeben sollst du mir die Erstgeburt, herausgeben sollst du mir Vater und Mutter ... (74)

From this primal act of betrayal everything else has followed directly and inescapably. From the beginning he has been trapped — Guelso sees — in a horrifying spiral of frustration and destructiveness. The more fiercely he has struggled to regain the love he has lost, the more his parents have recoiled from his fury; the greater his sense of outrage, the more violent the wrong they have inflicted on him (75). Looking back, however, he recognizes that all the frenzied hatred which now consumes him was latent in his violation as a helpless child, that everything else was merely confirmation. In his tenderest years it was already decreed that he must kill his brother at the appointed time (100).

Yet although Guelso is possessed by this terrible realisation he is unable to embrace it in his conscious mind. Indeed it so overpowers and confuses him that it threatens completely to undermine his sense of his own inner unity. All his encounters in the first half of the play (before the murder of Ferdinando) serve to show the depth of this spiritual disorientation. Although the action in the first three acts consists largely of a series of encounters between Guelso and other members of the family circle — his mother, father,

Ferdinando, Kamilla and his closest friend, Grimaldi – these do not mark any heightening of his passion or of his resolve, but reveal rather the fully consummated quality of his hatred. They illuminate from different points of view Guelso's state of utter subjection to his murderous frenzy: his absolute certainty that he must kill his brother and that this 'judgement' must be carried out on the day of Ferdinando's proposed marriage to Kamilla, the girl who (as Guelso believes) first loved him (97). In demonstrating Guelso's bondage to the violence within him these encounters also reveal his inability as a conscious, willing agent to embrace the implacable necessity which drives him. In all his confrontations with these other figures, as also in his private musings, we see him reel wildly between clashing sensations of strength and terror, fulfilment and break-down. No sooner is he borne aloft by the liberating force of his hatred which sweeps aside all injustice and oppression, than he recoils in dread from its disabling fury. At moments of ecstatic violence he feels his rage flow through him like a power of nature and senses his unity with a cosmic world beyond all human corruption (70; 78; 97). It is above all in his awareness of his passion as a renewing elemental force that Guelso feels his heroic selfhood as a man who transcends the world and bends it to his will.

This exultant experience of freeing power never persists, however. Before long it always gives way to a nightmare sense of horror from which Guelso cowers in terror. At times like this his anger seems to invade him like a curse, a sickness, a miasmic force of evil which cuts him off from the creative powers of life and drives him relentlessly towards a black abyss of madness (99). His rage far from granting freedom and fulfilment haunts him as a force of contagion and death. All the while as he awaits the inescapable carrying out of the dread act Guelso remains trapped in this racking inner confusion. Although nothing can shake his realisation that he must kill Ferdinando this realisation divides him against himself and robs him of all sustaining sense of inner coherence. Yet whether he embraces his passion with exultant pride or shrinks from it with horror he never wavers in the knowledge that he is the object of its implacable power.

Only in the execution of the act itself is Guelso carried beyond this crippling sense of inner disorientation and brought to the very brink of a new and terrible self-recognition. When he returns home after killing his brother, he appears not as the triumphant heir, the vindicated hero, but as a man spiritually unhinged by the force of a hatred which violates the deepest forces of his own being (115 ff.). In terror he sees the mark of Cain upon his brow and knows that he must live accursed and rejected by all men. In his final confrontation with his father he still fights, it is true, to hide the rising force of his despair. In submitting himself to Old Guelso's sentence of death, however, he yields to a spiritual desolation he can no longer resist.

In *Die Zwillinge* the dramatist is attempting to realise a more complex tragic conception than in his earlier plays. He is still intent on involving us directly and intensely in the subjective experience of the hero, but here he is also concerned at the same time to discredit Guelso's views of himself and his predicament by showing that he is unable to understand his own deepest feelings and aspirations. Through his very subtle analytical presentation Klinger succeeds in laying bare influences at work in the first formative years of Guelso's life which profoundly shape his experience in ways he himself cannot grasp. He is certainly aware that his lust for revenge is rooted in the shattering experience of parental rejection in early childhood. This awareness, however, far from opening the way to genuine self-knowledge has the effect of alienating him irrecoverably from his real self. For Guelso, as the dramatist makes clear, is unable to understand the essentially parasitic, perverting nature of his hatred: to see that its roots are in love, that its power reflects the force of the longing which has been denied. It becomes clear early in the action that the convulsive hatred which Guelso regards as proof of his heroic strength is in fact a symptom of a fundamental emotional dependence — a will to relatedness which is the primary impulse of his being.

This revelation of Guelso's failure to understand the nature of his hatred is crucial. It forces us to question his whole view of his familial situation and in particular of his lethal conflict with his brother. Guelso sees himself as involved principally in a struggle for social supremacy. Ferdinand, he believes, is the only impediment which stands in the way of the power, standing and scope which are his by right (21 f.; 103). By killing his brother he re-makes the world in keeping with his heroic image of himself — shapes it as a sphere in which he can express the strength, daring and enterprise which raise him above ordinary men. It is above all his readiness to assert his right to this new order even through the act of fratricide that is for him final proof of his inborn supremacy.

Klinger's probing, retrospective apprehension of the tragic crisis undermines this aspiration to heroic greatness. He shows that Guelso's hatred of Ferdinand is already fully formed in early child-hood and must now explode in murderous fury — whatever the circumstances of his adult life. This revelation of the coercive force of the hero's infantile experience has the effect of throwing into doubt any intellectual interpretation which he now as a grown man places upon his actions, and seems in particular to undermine his sense of the social significance of his conflict with Ferdinand. The deterministic impetus of Klinger's presentation seems here, as also in his earlier plays, to focus the close-knit sphere of family relationships as the real arena of the tragic crisis in a way which effectively severs it from the processes of the surrounding world. The tragic necessity in *Die Zwillinge* lies in Guelso's experience as a young child at the hands of his parents. It is noticeable, however, that Klinger does not attempt to show how this experience came into being. He does not explore what actually happened to Guelso, how his parents felt about him and treated him in these first crucial formative years, much less to relate this to their general view of life and moral out-look. Here, as in his earlier plays, Klinger refrains from outlining clearly the basic presuppositions of the tragic development, and this lack of firm exposition indicates once again his refusal to pin down and specify the causes of the hero's experience of discrepancy. His aim again is rather to present it as discontinuous with the working of contingent forces and in so doing, it seems, to lend it a wider, existential significance.

In *Die Zwillinge* Klinger it would appear, is intent on evoking a fundamental contradiction between the individual's inborn will to love and a world which thwarts and perverts this deepest impulse. Here again the dramatist's concern is noticeably restricted. He seeks to penetrate the tragic anguish of the hero and grasp in immediate, vibrant detail the ways in which he confronts the alien, self-destroy-ing rage which consumes him. This intense, inward vision of self-violation excludes, as I have tried to show, any significant socially critical concern. Klinger is not really out, as recent commentators like Huyssen and Kafitz have claimed[13], to condemn the law of primogeniture and through this to reject the individual's relation to the feudal state. The tendency of his vision is, I have suggested, to see tragic experience as essentially separate from social actuality; to see it as reflecting an antagonism between self and world which is metaphysical in origin and hence finally impenetrable.

109

IV

In all three plays Klinger explores a contradiction between the
innate creative energies of the individual and a situation which
thwarts and negates them. His tragic conception presupposes the
helpless exposure of the protagonist to destructive forces over
which he has no control, yet – as we have seen – the dramatist
does not attempt to grasp these as inherent in a clearly defined,
analysable situation. In none of these works does he see the external
determinants of the action as part of a pervading process of causation which constitutes the tragic necessity. He seems intent rather
on realising the hero's inward experience of contradiction as something which in its disabling depth and finality is incommensurable
with the working of contingent outer forces. There is, I believe, a
split in the conception of these works which Klinger himself does
not acknowledge. On the one hand, he is concerned to evoke a
discrepancy in the self which is ineluctable and finally mysterious,
and for these reasons, tragic. At the same time, however, although
he shows that this discrepancy is precipitated by circumstances in
the protagonists' environment, he tends to obscure this causal link,
apparently in the belief that in defining it he would in some way
undermine the transcendent significance he attributes to the experience of the tragic figure. Klinger's view of tragic suffering seems, in
other words, to resist the awareness of the individual's dependence
on circumstance which nonetheless shapes his conception of the
dramatic development.

The dramatist seems to have become more and more aware of
this tension in his tragic awareness in the months following the
completion of *Die Zwillinge* in 1775. This is clearly apparent, I
think, in his conception of the action in *Sturm und Drang* (1776) in
which he ironically points up the disparity between the passionate
experience of the characters and their actual situation as the source
of a powerful comic effect. The opening scenes of the play show
how the fierce youthful passion of Karoline Berkley and Karl Bushy
has been thwarted by the bitter feud which has erupted between
the two families (298 f.). Karoline, languishing in an American inn
with her brooding father, is aware that she is separated from her
lover not just by the ocean but by a hostility just as vast and implacable (311 ff.). Against all the odds, however, Karl Bushy turns
up at the inn followed, just as unaccountably, by his father soon

110

afterwards. The latter brings the miraculous revelation that the terrible conflict between the families is all a mistake, the results of a disastrous misunderstanding (345 ff.). It was not he who plotted the downfall of the Berkley family but another nameless individual now dead. All the mutual suspicion and hatred are the result of a fateful delusion which has engulfed both families and driven them to the very brink of a dreadful catastrophe. It is not too late, however. This supreme revelation is able to undo all the intensifying hostility and release the reconciliation for which both families have yearned in their heart of hearts – a reconciliation triumphantly vindicated in the joyous union of the lovers (348 f.).

It is impossible not to notice how clearly the development of the plot in *Sturm und Drang* mirrors the movement of the action in Klinger's earlier tragedies. The ironic aim of the comic development here, however, is to show that the destructive passions of the characters have no finality: they arise out of misunderstanding and can be overcome when this misunderstanding is destroyed. All the bitter antagonism which seemed to acquire a remorseless tragic momentum, has no basis in reality and can thus be thrown off by the dramatic figures who long subconsciously to resume their original creative ways of thinking and feeling. In thus exposing the crucial discrepancy between seemingly irrevocable passion and the situation out of which it arises, Klinger seems to be questioning ironically the notion of tragic necessity which governs the conception of his earlier plays. He seems in particular to be linking the incoherence in the comic plot to the social disconnectedness of the characters – relating the falsity of their passions to their crucial failure to understand their situation in society. Those agents who seek to foment conflict can pursue their machinations undisturbed and their evil purposes be attributed to others because neither family can grasp the nature of its involvement in corporate existence. The comic development shows how misapprehension of the real tensions shaping the life of society leads to the basic misunderstanding of themselves and others they claim to know and trust.

In this dark, disconcerting comedy Klinger seems to be groping, albeit obliquely, towards a new notion of tragic necessity. Necessity – as he here seems to envisage it – does not lie solely in the impelling momentum of passions in the inward self, but stems rather from the organic interaction between the individual and his situation – an interaction which he seems intent on seeing as a pervasive process of causality. Klinger attempted to confront imaginatively this fuller and more complex awareness of tragedy in *Die neue Arria*. Here for the first time he presents a tragic action which reflects, openly and in some detail, the involvement of the characters in a particular political-social situation and which seeks to grasp a corporate dimension of significance. The central contradiction in this work does not spring (as in his earlier plays) from tensions in the closed sphere of family relationships but grows out of a collision between this sphere, and the values and responsibilities it entails, and the alien world of political power and control.

At the beginning of the action in *Die neue Arria* Julio, the central figure, appears as a man deeply at odds with himself. He feels driven on the one hand by an urge to total self-realisation which he has no means of expressing and is yet at the same time aware that his love for the withdrawn, madonna-like Laure inhibits his possibilities of growth. For all his yearning for a fulfilment which would raise him above his day-to-day existence he sees that his love binds him to the narrower world he would transcend. It is clear that at this stage Julio can understand fulfilment only in terms of a limitless assertion of the self:

> Ich will alles tun, da soll nichts über mir noch um mich dazu helfen, als ich ... Lieber mein Leben bei der Erde geblieben, als einer fremden Macht was zu verdanken zu haben. (136)

Julio's predicament lies in the fact that this egoistic will to fulfilment which he affirms as the deepest impulse of his being, remains unfocussed and confused and in conflict with his love for Laure which is the only emotional experience possessing him. It is only when he comes face to face with the masterful, passionate Solina that Julio is able to break out of this disabling contradiction. His encounter with her has the effect of releasing a new, transforming awareness of himself which eclipses at a stroke his anxious devotion to Laure and opens up the vision of a supreme destiny which surpasses all his earlier experience. The love which now seizes possession of him draws together all his separate, warring impulses in a sublime commitment which renews and fulfils his being. Solina inspires in Julio a passion in which heroic will and self-giving are fused in one ultimate purpose. Under her transforming influence Julio undergoes the crucial recognition that his love for her is not an emotion complete in itself and separable from the rest of his existence, but rather a force which in its vital power must transform his awareness of the world in which he lives, and that in the most immediate and demanding way (139 ff.). For love in this highest form, as Solina forces him to see, involves a moral obligation he cannot evade; in his particular situation it demands that he dedicate himself to the overthrow of the evil tyrannical Prince Galbino who has seized power through treachery and murder, and now subjects the state to a ruthless reign of terror (160 ff.).

Klinger stresses the supreme synthesizing significance of Julio's undertaking. His passionate moral idealism is fired by his love for Solina and at the same time by his sense of a deep personal loyalty to Kornelia, the widow of the murdered Duke Aemilius who now lives alone and in terror of the sadistic Galbino (163 f.). His view of the renewed and liberated state culminates in the vision of the Herzogin restored to her rightful place on the throne which she holds in trust for the son of her dead husband. Julio's leadership of the uprising — as Klinger is concerned to show — is both an intensely heroic purpose and a supreme moral commitment. The dramatist makes it clear that in this severe corporate crisis only the inspired leadership of the outstanding individual can hold together the different factions and mount a sustained impetus of revolt. At the same time Klinger shows that only this total sacrificial dedication to the good of the state has the sublimity adequate to Julio's yearning for supeme heroic fulfilment.

The playwright succeeds admirably in my view in revealing the driving intensity of Julio's leadership and in showing how deeply his commitment to the revolt is bound up with this new awareness of power and freedom released in him by Solina's love. It seems to me, however, that this revelation of the force of Julio's sexual longing has consequences which Klinger does not intend. It has the effect of undermining the inherent political-moral significance which he is explicitly attributing to the hero's opposition to Galbino. In the end, in fact, Julio's will to destroy the usurper appears more and more clearly as a symptom of his infatuation — of a need to prove himself worthy of the masterful woman who utterly possesses him. His commitment to the revolt, far from demonstrating the assertive freedom of the hero, reveals an emotional dependence so profound that he cannot acknowledge it for what it is.

The fatal weakness of Klinger's presentation here is that he fails to show Julio as capable of genuine political concern. The hero seems simply to absorb from Solina a passionate desire to overthrow Galbino and never shows himself capable of assimilating this desire to a broader vision of a more just and ordered state. The force with which the dramatist lays bare the sexual roots of Julio's heroic yearning contrives, it seems to me, to rob the whole action of a valid political dimension and thus to isolate the central sphere of tragic experience from the wider world of actual historical conditions. This separation is most evident in Klinger's concern to present the climax as triumphant and reconciliatory. He portrays the resolve of the lovers to die together after the failure of the revolt rather than submit to a life apart from one another as a proof of the power of their love to free them from the grip of arbitrary, destructive circumstance (197 ff.). This affirmation of the liberating power of love serves, however, to negate the historical significance of the revolt, to reduce it to a mere foil to the transcendent passion of the lovers. For this attempt to see the deaths of Julio and Solina as the vehicle of a final reconciliation which transfigures the whole dramatic action involves a complete disregard of the wider corporate world – a world stricken by the consequences of the failed revolt. It deflects attention from the fact that the sadistic, treacherous Galbino still wields unfettered power over the state, that justice and order are no nearer than at the beginning of the play.

V

In their eagerness to put forward a clear-cut, coherent view of Klinger's work, his critics have generally failed, it seems to me, to do justice to the elusive, deeply paradoxical character of his tragic awareness. They have failed in particular to grasp the essential ambiguity of the ferocious destructive passions of his heroic protagonists. The convulsive quest for vengeance and murder which takes possession of figures like Otto, Wild or Guelso appears in Klinger's perception of tragedy as inherently two-faced and contradictory. For in revealing the supreme passionate power which raises them above ordinary men the dramatist also shows the depth of the violation they have suffered, the immensity of their victimisation.

Klinger sees his heroes as driven by a primal in-born will to love. This will, as the playwright presents it, is so fundamental, so impelling that it cannot be suppressed or reduced by the external forces which deny it expression. When it is thwarted this deepest energy in the self swings round into a raging lust to destroy which in its blind fury reveals the full force of the creative impulse which has been frustrated.

The playwright, as I have stressed, seems intent on showing the tragic process as inherent in the underived, metaphysical selfhood of the heroic protagonist. Figures like Otto or Guelso preside over this process but do not participate in it as responsible and effective moral agents. It is not just that they have no control over their elemental need for love; they are equally helpless before the processes through which it is perverted into unbridled, self-destroying hatred. Klinger seems to perceive the tragic development as enacting a contradiction between the essential personhood of the hero, what constitutes his supreme individuality, and a world which is inescapably in conflict with it. Klinger's attempts to dramatise what he clearly regarded as a metaphysical, and thus mysterious and insoluble, discrepancy between self and world constantly involve him in the acknowledgement of the power of concrete social forces over the individual's existence, although he constantly refuses to define these explicitly. Pervading his plays is a strong latent awareness of the driving momentum of society, of its specific, inexorable structures and assumptions, which was averse to his conscious tragic aims and from which he seems consistently to recoil.

Chapter VI

SCHILLER AND AFTER.
THE STURM UND DRANG AND THE DEVELOPMENT
OF GERMAN DRAMA

I

1776 marks both the climax and the effective end of the drama of the Sturm und Drang. This year saw the appearance of some of its best known and influential plays – *Die Zwillinge, Die neue Arria, Sturm und Drang, Die Soldaten, Die Kindermörderin* as well as Leisewitz's *Julius von Tarent*. After this the movement produced no play of any significance and began to lose its creative impetus. Over the years, it is true, commentators have tended to regard the early plays of Schiller like *Die Räuber* (1781) and *Kabale und Liebe* (1784) as extending and renewing the drama of the Sturm und Drang in the next decade.[1] This is a long-standing view which still enjoys wide critical acceptance; it seems to me, however, to rest upon a misunderstanding both of the drama of the 1770's and of the distinctive shaping impulses of Schiller's early work. In the following comments I would like just to summarise an argument I have developed in detail elsewhere,[2] and use it as a starting-point for an assessment of the historical situation of the drama of the Sturm und Drang as a whole.

Schiller does not in my view extend the drama of the 1770's in the sense of developing organic new dramatic forms, but takes over rather some of its innovative concerns and methods as a means of confronting and clarifying his own essential imaginative preoccupations. We can see the influence of the Sturm und Drang on both *Die Räuber* and *Kabale und Liebe*, especially in Schiller's view of the confrontation of the heroic protagonist with an alien, destructive society. This analytical perception does not, however, fully embody the central impetus of his creative preoccupation which is to apprehend the relation of the dramatic agents to a transcendent moral order – a concern quite foreign to the drama of the Sturm und Drang. The rift between empirical, social insight and visionary ethical awareness is very evident in *Die Räuber* where it threatens to undermine the unity of the tragic structure. At the very heart of

117

Schiller's creative interest here is the predicament of the heroic idealist, Karl Moor, who is thrust from supreme metaphysical assurance into devouring nihilistic despair by the belief that his father has rejected him.[3] The fissure in the play's conception stems from Schiller's attempt to express this absolute moral disillusion in terms of Moor's rebellion against the corrupt society in which he lives: to see his despair as embodied in the hero's attempt to overthrow oppression and injustice (515 f.). The despair which engulfs Moor, however, resists all such revolutionary aspirations. The dramatist shows in the opening act that Moor's belief in his father's betrayal releases in him a disintegrating vision of a world driven by egotism and violence – a world ultimately corrupt and irredeemable (514 ff.). After the end of the second act Schiller tends, in fact, to detach his hero more and more from his social environment and to focus all his attention on the process of Moor's moral regeneration. Karl Moor's realisation that he has been betrayed not by his father but by his malevolent, plotting brother Franz, that his father never ceased to love him, is the beginning of his renewal. It restores his belief in a providential, morally significant universe and asserts quite unambiguously the supremacy of the visionary, methphysical perspective (581 f.; 610 f.). This is quite clear in the way Schiller presents the deaths of the two brothers at the end of the play. The despairing suicide of the amoral egotist, Franz, like the willed, expiatory surrender of Karl affirms the ultimate power and significance of the moral law and the judgement which awaits all men (617 f.). This tragic climax eclipses all relative historical-social circumstances. The law to which Karl Moor gives his life no longer appears as the vehicle of a corrupt, oppressive society against which he had taken up arms, but as the symbol of a transcendent ethical order from which human existence derives its ultimate significance.

In *Kabale und Liebe* the playwright attempts once again to assimilate an analytical view of the tragic development to a quest for supreme moral significance. In the extensive, probing exposition he lays bare a crisis which seems to rise directly out of the deep antagonisms of the contemporary world. He is concerned to show that the predicament of the lovers, Ferdinand, the son of the President, and Luise, the daughter of a lower middle-class musician, is inherent in their involvement in a tense, divided society which undermines their search for love in ways they cannot fully understand (765 ff.; 807 ff.). Luise in her passive, conforming rootedness is simply

118

unable to respond to the imperious determination of Ferdinand to sweep aside all inherited ties and responsibilities in order to fulfil his passion. In her bondage to home, family and the prevailing social order she recoils helplessly before his reckless belief in his right to create his life as he alone wills it.

As the action develops, however, the protagonists seem to outgrow the determining pressures of their social identities and to assert their ultimate moral selfhood. When, for instance, Ferdinand the outraged lover, claims the right to kill the girl who, he believes, has betrayed him, he no longer appears simply as a self-willed, demanding aristocrat but as a man before God. Face to face with the Creator he demands the right, which he knows is His alone, to take Luise's life even though he knows this will mean his eternal damnation (822). Similarly at the climax of the tragic action the Luise who sublimely forgives her murderer is no longer the constrained and vulnerable middle-class girl of the opening acts. She appears here as a moral being who transcends all the restrictions and inhibitions imposed on her by her narrow middle-class background, and who is able to see her whole life in the light of eternity (855 f.).

There can be no doubt that Schiller's encounter with the drama of the Sturm und Drang did have a deep impact on the conception of his early plays. This is most obviously apparent in his view of the heroic individual as the antagonist of society, as challenging its injustice and corruption in the name of higher moral imperatives. But this social concern, I have suggested, is not finally compatible with his determining tragic perception of the dramatic figures as agents who shape their destinies in a moral universe which makes supreme, unquestionable demands upon them. Schiller's preoccupation with the predicament of the heroic rebel drives him to articulate what are essentially religious and ethical conflicts in terms of relative social antagonisms, and this (I have argued) tends to impede and subvert the visionary drive of his creative imagination. After completing *Kabale und Liebe* it is noticeable that he abandons his attempts to integrate socially critical analysis with visionary ethical idealism. In his hard struggle with this work, it would seem, he realised more and more clearly that his tragic imagination needed the scope and freedom which were incompatible with the intense social concern characteristic of his first plays.

II

This brief discussion of the relations between Schiller's early work and the plays of the 1770's gives us, I think, a helpful starting-point for an exploration of the place of the Sturm und Drang in the development of German drama. Like the Naturalists at the end of the 19th century the writers of the Sturm und Drang were attempting to effect a revolution in the drama. Consciously and unconsciously they were intent on realising conceptions of the drama which were incompatible with the basic assumptions of classicist dramaturgy. In this sense their plays were essentially experimental. This is most obvious in the force of the analytical impulse which informs their works — an impulse that is basically at odds with the Aristotelian view of the drama as a supremely personal, integrated form which Lessing had recently re-stated with such authority in the *Hamburgische Dramaturgie*. The drama, as Lessing defines it here, is a dynamic, rigorously coherent mode which embodies a vision of man's moral existence as sequential, purposive action. The whole process of action in the drama, he insists, is initiated and fulfilled by moral agents, and this interpersonal action is the conclusive expression of a total dramatic world. In it all the latent energies of the hero's moral self and all the inherent tensions in his sustaining relationships come to effective realisation. The dramatic situation, as he saw it, embraced subjective will and opposing force in taut, inescapable correlation.[4] Here every movement in the inward self had some impact upon the surrounding world, while every outward occurence necessarily affected the consciousness of the character. In the world of the drama the purpose of the individual did not exist independently of his capacity to act, just as the circumstances of his environment were real only to the extent that they had a bearing upon the unfolding of his purpose.[5]

This view of the dramatic world as an arena of tense, interlocking forces underlies all Lessing's thinking on the drama. His discussions of action constantly assume that the interchange between self and world can be articulated as one necessary, coherent development: that the inner drive of the self towards action, the effects of the committed act on the existing situation, its repercussions upon the agent — that these constitute together one single, integrated process of causation. His sense of the coherence of the dramatic form stems from the assumption of a close mutuality between the inward life of the dramatic figures and the circumstances by which they are bound; and this in turn rests upon the primary presupposition of an organic, morally significant relationship between self and world as the very basis of the dramatic structure.

The empirical, probing awareness of the playwrights of the Sturm und Drang is fundamentally at odds with this conception of the self-sufficient integrity of the dramatic form. If we consider, for instance, Goethe's *Götz* which marks a decisive step towards a new order of dramatic realism, it is immediately evident how far the analytical concern of the playwright extends beyond the specific events depicted on stage and seeks to place them in a wide, qualifying context. Goethe develops here new discriminating expository methods in order to grasp the political-social, economic and religious tensions which determine existence in the German states in the late 16th century. He is intent on showing that the interplay of these forces is so intricate and ambiguous that none of the dramatic figures can understand much less control it.

These analytical procedures pioneered by Goethe are taken up and refined in the works of Lenz and Wagner who seek to give a closely detailed, incisive analysis of existence in contemporary society. Both playwrights demonstrate that the conflicts they present grow out of the deep-lying antagonisms which rend the whole social structure. Both are intent on exposing the forces of prejudice, resentment and fear which divide the different social groups and affect the responses of the individual figures to one another in ways they themselves cannot comprehend. In works like *Der Hofmeister* or *Die Kindermörderin*, for instance, the dramatist shows how the characters are driven into conflict by forces beyond their personal awareness or control — a conflict for which they are quite unprepared and with which they cannot cope.

In these and other works of the Sturm und Drang the individual figure stands, it seems to me, in a quite new relationship to the total world of the play. He appears in a fundamental way as entrapped, the object of an overwhelming, impenetrable environment, forced to act out his existence in a world beyond the scope of his understanding or effective influence. The dynamic aspiring Götz as much as the oppressed, bewildered Stolzius appears in the end as driven by remorseless impersonal processes which transcend the immediate sphere of the dramatic development and which the playwright can illustrate but not enact. This is, I think, characteristic of the extent to which the young dramatists of the Sturm und Drang were reaching out towards quite new analytical, realistic conceptions of the drama — conceptions which seem to anticipate the kind of empirical awareness which Hettner in 1851 saw as the prerogative of contemporary drama:

> Das Schicksal thront nicht mehr über und außer der Welt, das Schicksal ist nichts Anderes als die herrschende Weltlage selber, von der jeder Einzelne abhängt; es sind die aus dieser Weltlage entspringenden Sitten, Begriffe und Zustände, die für den Einzelnen als Einzelnen durchaus undurchbrechbar und deshalb für ihn eine tragische Macht sind.[6]

The strong analytical drive informing the conception of the plays of the Sturm und Drang is finally incompatible with the integrity of the dramatic form as this had been traditionally understood. In fact, the playwrights seem bent on grasping the dramatic action in terms of a fundamental discontinuity: on counterposing an external sphere of social causality with a subjective world of personal awareness and aspiration. These works seek at once to define the empirical forces which determine the momentum of the action, and to evoke the inward experience of the individual protagonist in a way which lends it a powerful dramatic force and significance. In plays as outwardly different as the *Urfaust* or *Die Zwillinge, Die Kindermörderin* or *Otto* we can see this far-reaching attempt to internalise the action, to apprehend developments, as it were, through the eyes of the isolated individual figure. The dramatists are here all concerned in their different ways to grasp the tensions in the withdrawn self as an unfolding process of inner crisis which has its own impetus and necessity and which, as the play develops, comes more and more to shape the imaginative impact of the work as a whole.

Underlying this quest for a new dramatic inwardness we can see a strong impulse, characteristic of the drama of the Sturm und Drang, to assert the subjective world of the self as a sphere of value in its own right which is inescapably at odds with the depersonalised, destructive world of corporate existence. The individual, though engulfed in this impenetrable, alien world and largely deprived of the possibility of effective action, still appears here as a being capable of significant inward experience. The anguished, divided self, torn between longing and conditioned fear, hope and

122

repression is apprehended in these works as a centre of fraught, sensitive awareness which is a source of intense tragic interest and concern. These playwrights of the Sturm und Drang would have shared Lessing's impatience with those critics who saw action only in terms of vulgar external collision:

> Es hat ihnen nie beifallen wollen, daß auch jeder innere Kampf von Leidenschaften, jede Folge von verschiedenen Gedanken, wo eine die andere aufhebt, eine Handlung sei.[7]

This probing, insistent attempt to grasp the fundamental discrepancy between self and world as the basis of a new dramatic form is, as I see it, the most innovative and certainly prophetic impulse in the drama of the Sturm und Drang. The young playwrights succeeded in opening up possibilities of tragedy which were immediately rooted in the actual experience of living in society and were in keeping with the increasingly secular, empirical awareness of the late 18th century. None of the dramatists offered a clear theoretical definition of his aims but we can see that they were intuitively reaching out towards a new kind of relative or qualified tragedy – a mode which could no longer claim the universal, metaphysical significance of classicist forms but which still sought the shattering emotional impact peculiar to tragedy.

Friedrich Hebbel was one of the first critics to note the relativity of this conception. In his foreword to *Maria Magdalena* (1844) he attempted to analyze and discredit it. He pointed out that the action in the social dramas of the Sturm und Drang is finally dependent upon the conditions of contemporary society and is therefore incapable of embodying the ultimate, timeless order of necessity essential to tragedy; it was always possible to see the characters in these plays as existing in different circumstances, and say 'if only'.[8]

From the point of view of his own philosophical convictions Hebbel gives in fact a highly perceptive critical diagnosis of the conception of some of the most characteristic works of the Sturm und Drang. He does not see them historically, however. He fails to do justice to the questioning, pragmatic concerns of the playwrights in the 1770's – to the urgency of their experimental attempts to come to terms with their own lived experience. Above all it fails to take account of the fact that their aim was often precisely to grasp the contingency of the individual's relationship to his social environment as the basis of a new tragic structure. The dramatists did, it is true, seek to lay bare the causal link between the predicament of the tragic figures and the constraining pressures of social existence and in this respect were intent on demonstrating a kind of inevitability. But they were in their different ways also at pains to suggest that these social determinants lacked final, metaphysical necessity; that they manifested inequities or failures in the life of society which would be overcome by the processes of historical development. Hebbel, who remained deeply rooted in the classical tragic tradition, clearly could not respond to the questioning, exploratory drive informing these works, and could only regard the profound tensions in their conception as a symptom of disabling incoherence. And in fact it is doubtful if the playwrights themselves were fully aware of the deeply dissonant effect which their works really entailed. For they were intent on presenting a spectacle of suffering which in one perspective seems unavoidable and thus evokes sympathy and imaginative acceptance, but which in another seems to flow from circumstances which are transient and surmountable, and thus drives the spectator to dissatisfaction and protest. This clash of imaginative perspectives shapes in a quite disconcerting way the presentation of the catastrophe in *Götz von Berlichingen*. This forces us to respond at once to the reconciling personal tragedy of the hero and to the vision of the immense, senseless suffering of the oppressed German people which extends far beyond the limits of the dramatic action. A similarly perplexing interplay of religious and socially critical view-points also informs Goethe's apprehension of the death of Gretchen in *Urfaust*. Just as unsettling in a rather different way, however, is the persistent attempt of Lenz in his comedies to confront an awareness of the remorseless social subjection of the individual with a recognition of his profound impulsive and emotional energies which precede and surpass his environmentally controlled existence.

Wagner, it seems to me, takes this two-fold, dissonant mode of perception a stage further and seeks to exploit it as a means of a quite explicit propagandist purpose. In *Die Kindermörderin* in particular he involves the spectator intensely in the suffering of Evchen and draws him to experience her spiritual break-down as inescapable. The ending of the play goes beyond this catastrophe, however. It does not annul the profound sympathy which the spectacle of

124

Evchen's suffering evokes, but seeks rather to impose upon it a summons to reject the injustice, oppression and sheer inhumanity of the society which both bears the responsibility for her inner collapse and seeks to condemn her for it. The catastrophe which in the context of the social conditions in Straßburg in the 1770's appears as inevitable, is exposed by this ending as arbitrary and intolerable. Gröningseck's quest to have the mandatory death-sentence on Evchen repealed has a powerfully symbolic force. The spectator is here challenged, like Gröningseck, to assert himself against the rampant injustice and cruelty which blight the life of society — to commit himself actively to the creation of a new and better order.

This exploratory quest to embrace conflicting view-points and insights — to evoke the remorseless necessity of tragedy while analyzing its roots in contingent social circumstances — this is characteristic in one way or another of all the powerful plays of the Sturm und Drang. It represents, I believe, a break-through of great historical importance for the development of German drama. In fact, it seems to me to anticipate all the main attempts to develop new, more realistic forms of tragedy for over a century. This concern to apprehend the individual protagonist at once as a determinate social being and as a significant tragic subject is, for instance, at the very heart of the attempts of the young German dramatists like Gutzkow, and Laube and Marggraff in the 1840's to develop a new kind of dissident political tragedy.[9] It also impels in a different way Büchner's revolutionary attempt to fuse virulent social indictment and intense tragic awareness in his fragment *Woyzeck* (1837) — a fragment influenced, as critics have long acknowledged, by the playwright's long, intense involvement with the work of Lenz.[10]

It is, however, only with the development of Naturalism in the 1890's that the search for a radical, socially committed realism assumes a completely dominant importance in the drama. Commentators like Kühnemann, Brahm, Schlenther and Halbe who attempted to work out theories of the new drama were all concerned to show that its roots lay not in France but in their own national literary tradition and especially in the Sturm und Drang. The crucial achievement of Ibsen, as these and other critics saw it, lay in the fact that he was the first modern playwright to integrate a powerful individualistic preoccupation with a rigorous empirical awareness in a tense, theatrically effective dramatic form. Ibsen in creating this

125

challenging 'scientific' drama had also, they believed, brought to the forefront of critical concern a vital tradition in German drama which had been largely neglected by critics dedicated to the preservation of the obsolete classicist tradition throughout the 19th century.[11] There can be little doubt that the Naturalists would have seen the attempts of playwrights like Brecht, Hacks and Kipphardt in our own century to adapt and renew works of the Sturm und Drang as a substantial vindication of their view.[12]

NOTES

Notes to Introduction

1 Wilhelm Scherer, *Geschichte der deutschen Literatur*, 2nd ed. (Berlin, 1884), pp. 470 ff.
Erich Schmidt, *Lenz und Klinger. Zwei Dichter der Geniezeit*, (Berlin, 1878), pp. 6 ff.
For a full and perceptive historical survey of the critical reception of the Sturm und Drang see Andreas Huyssen, *Drama des Sturm und Drang* (München, 1980), pp. 13 ff.

2 The most influential example of this is Heinz Kindermann, *Jakob Michael Reinhold Lenz und die deutsche Romantik* (Wien, 1925).

3 Georg Lukács, *Faust und Faustus. Ausgewählte Schriften*, Vol. 2 (Reinbek, 1967), pp. 13 ff.
Heinz Stolpe, *Die Auffassung des jungen Herder vom Mittelalter*, (Weimar, 1955), pp. 4 ff.
Edith Braemer, *Goethes Prometheus und die Grundpositionen des Sturm und Drang* (Weimar, 1963), pp. 20 ff.

4 See Huyssen, op. cit., pp. 27 ff.

5 Walter Hinck ed., *Sturm und Drang. Ein literaturwissenschaftliches Studienbuch* (Kronberg/Ts., 1978)
Otto Dann, *Epoche – sozialgeschichtlicher Abriß*, in *Deutsche Literatur. Eine Sozialgeschichte*, ed. Horst Albert Glaser. Vol. 4, *Zwischen Absolutismus und Aufklärung 1740 - 1786*, ed. Ralph-Rainer Wuthenow, (Reinbek, 1980), pp. 12-25.
Horst Albert Glaser, *Drama des Sturm und Drang*, in Wuthenow op. cit., pp. 299-322.
Jochen Schulte-Sasse, *Poetik und Ästhetik Lessings und seiner Zeigenossen*, in *Deutsche Aufklärung bis zur Französischen Revolution*, ed. Rolf Grimminger, *Hansers Sozialgeschichte der deutschen Literatur*, Vol. 3 (München, 1980), pp. 304-326.
Gerhard Sauder, *Geniekult im Sturm und Drang*, in Grimminger, op. cit., pp. 327-340.
Bengt Algot Sørensen, *Herrschaft und Zärtlichkeit. Der Patriarchalismus und das Drama im 18. Jahrhundert* (München, 1984), is one of the rare studies which makes a highly productive attempt to combine historical-social investigation with close literary critical analysis.

6 Heinrich Wilhelm von Gerstenberg, *Briefe über Merkwürdigkeiten der Literatur*, 14. 18. und 20. Brief in *Sturm und Drang. Dichtungen und theoretische Texte*, ed. Heinz Nicolai (München, 1971), Vol. 1 p. 117.

Notes to Chapter one

1 See J.G. Robertson, *Lessings Dramatic Theory* (Cambridge, 1939) pp. 351 ff.

2 See especially Paul Böckmann, *Der dramatische Perspektivismus in der Shakespeare-Deutung des 18. Jahrhunderts*, in *Formensprache. Studien zur Literaturästhetik und Dichtungsinterpretation* (Hamburg, 1966), pp. 45 ff. Fritz Martini, *Die Poetik des Dramas im Sturm und Drang* in *Geschichte im Drama – Drama in der Geschichte* (Stuttgart, 1979), pp. 37-79.

3 Hertha Isaacsen, *Der junge Herder und Shakespeare* (Berlin, 1930), pp. 8 ff.; Huyssen, op. cit., pp. 96 ff.

4 Theodor Friedrich, *Die Anmerkungen übers Theater des Dichters Jakob Michael Reinhold Lenz* (Leipzig, 1909), pp. 37 ff. Eva Maria Inbar, *Shakespeare in Deutschland: Der Fall Lenz* (Tübingen, 1982), pp. 3 ff.

5 Edward McInnes, *Louis-Sébastian Mercier and the Drama of the Sturm und Drang*, Proceedings of the English Goethe Society, Vol. 54 (1984), pp. 76-100.

6 Huyssen, op. cit., pp. 99 f.

7 References to the *Hamburgische Dramaturgie* are to *Lessings Werke*, ed. J. Petersen and W. von Olshausen (Berlin, 1925 ff.). Vol. 5 pp. 325 ff.; See Robertson, op. cit., p. 245.

8 Gerstenberg, op. cit., pp. 56 ff.

9 J.G. Herders, *Sämtliche Werke*, ed. B. Suphan (Berlin, 1891), Vol. V, p. 231.

10 Roy Pascal, *The German Sturm und Drang* (Manchester, 1953), pp. 256 ff. Böckmann, op. cit., pp. 45 f.

11 Alexander Gillies, *Herders Essay on Shakespeare: Das Herz der Untersuchung*, *Modern Language Review*, 32 (1937), pp. 262-280.

12 J.M.R. Lenz, *Werke und Schriften*, ed. B. Titel und H. Haug, 2 vols. (Stuttgart, 1966 f.). *Anmerkungen übers Theater* and other critical and theoretical writings are in vol. 1; the plays are in vol. 2.

13 Inbar, op. cit., pp. 29 ff.

14 W.W. Pusey, *Louis-Sébastian Mercier in Germany* (New York, 1939), pp. 25 ff.

15 Louis-Sébastian Mercier, *Du Théatre. Nouvel Essai sur l'art dramatique* (Amsterdam, 1773), pp. 9 ff.

16 Peter Szondi, *Die Theorie des bürgerlichen Trauerspiels im 18. Jahrhundert* (Frankfurt am Main, 1974), pp. 168 ff.

Notes to chapter two

1 Friedrich Sengle, *Das deutsche Geschichtsdrama. Geschichte eines literarischen Mythos* (Stuttgart, 1952), p. 27.

2 Benno von Wiese, *Die deutsche Tragödie von Lessing bis Hebbel*, 2nd ed. (Hamburg, 1952), p. 64.
Emil Staiger, *Goethe, Vol. 1*, (Zürich, 4th ed. 1964), p. 85.
Wolfgang Kayser, introduction to *Götz von Berlichingen, Goethes Werke* Hamburger Ausgabe, Vol. 4, pp. 484 ff. All references to the play are to this edition.

3 Ilse Graham, *Götz von Berlichingen's Right Hand, German Life and Letters*, 16, (1963) pp. 212-228.
Frank Ryder, *Towards a Revaluation of Goethe's 'Götz'*, P.M.L.A. 77 (1962), pp. 58-70 and 79 (1964), pp. 58-66.

4 Fritz Martini, *Götz von Berlichingen. Charakterdrama und Gesellschaftsdrama*, in Martini, op. cit., pp. 104-128.

5 Martini, op. cit., 104 ff.

6 Recent interpretations by Rainer Nägele, *Götz von Berlichingen. Eine Geschichte und ihre Rekonstruktion*, in *Neue Interpretationen zu Goethes Dramen*, ed. Walter Hinderer (Stuttgart, 1980), pp. 65-77, and Huyssen, op. cit. pp. 130-156, attempt to assimilate the insights of Graham & Ryder and at the same time to extend Martini's view of the play as a 'social drama'. Volker Neuhaus, *'Götz von Berlichingen' in Geschichte als Schauspiel* ed. Walter Hinck (Frankfurt am Main, 1981), pp. 82-100, investigates the historical circumstances underlying the dramatic action in a very provocative and fruitful way. He comes in the end, however, to a view of the relation between the dramatic development and historical process which is in important aspects at odds with the interpretation put forward here.

7 Neuhaus, op. cit., pp. 90 ff., seriously underestimates the expository significance of these scenes and sees the introduction of the Roman legal system almost exclusively from the point of view of the hero. It is characteristic of the tendency of his interpretation that he relegates the Emperor to the status of an 'Episodenfigur'.

8 See Martini, op. cit., p. 115.

9 See Ursula Wertheim, *Die Helferstein-Szene in Goethes 'Urgötz' und ihre Beziehungen zum Volkslied, Weimarer Beiträge*, 1 (1955), pp. 112-143.

10 See Martini, op. cit., pp. 120 ff.

11 See Huyssen, pp. 135 ff.

Notes to chapter three

1 See above, pp. 25 ff.

2 Inbar, op. cit., pp. 46 ff.

3 Huyssen, op. cit., pp. 157 ff.

4 The two most fundamental and far-reaching interpretations of Lenz's plays as a new kind of tragi-comedy are:
K.S. Guthke, *Geschichte und Poetik der deutschen Tragikomödie* (Göttingen, 1961), pp. 55-77; R. Girard, *Lenz 1751 - 1792. Genèse d'une Dramaturgie du Tragi-Comique* (Paris, 1968).
See also John Osborne, *J.M.R. Lenz. The Renunciation of Heroism* (Göttingen, 1975), esp. pp. 100 ff.; John Guthrie, *Lenz and Büchner: Studies in dramatic Form* (Frankfurt a.M., 1984), pp. 53 ff.; Bruce Duncan, *The comic Structure of Lenz's 'Soldaten'* in *Modern Language Notes*, 91 (1976), pp. 515-523.

5 Titel & Haug, op. cit., vol. 2, pp. 727 ff.

6 Leo Kreutzer, *Literatur als Einmischung: J.M.R. Lenz*, in Hinck, *Sturm und Drang*, pp. 213-229; Guthrie, op. cit., pp. 53 ff.

7 Michael Butler, *Character and Paradox in Lenz's 'Der Hofmeister'*, *German Life and Letters*, 32, (1979), pp. 95-103.

8 Duncan, op. cit., pp. 515 ff.

9 Edward McInnes, *J.M.R. Lenz 'Die Soldaten'* (München, 1977), pp. 97 ff.

10 idem, pp. 117 f.

11 This development in the action seems to conform to the conception of comedy put forward, for instance, by Northorp Frey, *Anatomy of Criticism* (Princeton, 1951), pp. 180 ff.

12 Titel and Haug, *Lenz*, op. cit., vol. 2, pp. 737 f.

13 Osborne, op. cit., pp. 148 ff.

14 Karl Freye and Wolfgang Stammler, *Briefe von und an J.M.R. Lenz* (Leipzig, 1918), Vol. 1, p. 145.

15 idem, p. 115.

16 M.N. Rosanow, *Jakob M.R. Lenz, der Dichter der Sturm und Drang-Periode* (Leipzig, 1909), pp. 239 ff.

17 Kreutzer, op. cit., pp. 221 f.

18 McInnes, op. cit., pp. 97 ff.

19 Note how the Gräfin expresses her disbelief that Marie should have expectted to marry Desportes 'Wo dachten Sie hinaus? wo dachten Ihre Eltern hinaus?' (227).

20 Dieter Kafitz, *Grundzüge einer Geschichte des deutschen Dramas von Lessing bis zum Naturalismus* (Königstein/Ts., 1982), pp. 58 ff.

21 McInnes, op. cit., pp. 95 f.

Notes to chapter four

1 For a comprehensive study of this whole question see Alois Wierlacher, *Das bürgerliche Drama*, (München, 1968), pp. 64 ff.

2 Karl S. Guthke, *Das deutsche bürgerliche Trauerspiel*, 3rd ed. (Stuttgart, 1980), pp. 45 ff.

3 Wierlacher op. cit., pp. 66 f. Karl Eibl, *Lessing. Miss Sara Sampson* (Frankfurt a.M., 1971), pp. 138 ff.

4 Denis Diderot, *Oeuvres Esthétique* (Paris, 1959), p. 91.

5 See Guthke, op. cit., pp. 44 f.

6 I have discussed this in detail in *Lessing's 'Hamburgische Dramaturgie' and the Theory of the Drama in the 19th Century*, Oribs Litterarum 28 (1973) pp. 293-318.

7 Kafitz, op. cit., pp. 59 ff.

8 All references to Mercier's play are to Louis-Sébastian Mercier, *Théâtre Complet* (Amsterdam, 1778-84). *Le Deserteur* is in Vol. 1 *Le Faux Ami* and *Le Juge* in Vol. 2; *La Brouette du Vinaigrier* in Vol. 3, *Zoé* in Vol. 4.

9 It is characteristic eg. that Guthke, op. cit.; pp. 77 ff., follows most other surveys of domestic drama in this period in avoiding discussion of the *Urfaust*.

10 Eudo C. Mason, *Goethe's Faust. Its Genesis and Purport* (Berkley, 1969), pp. 194 ff., is one of the few critics who has written perceptively on the problems which faced Goethe in "adopting the theme of the seduced and infanticidal girl of the humbler classes to the requirements of the Faust-legend" (p. 197).

11   Mason, idem, pp. 198 ff.

12   See above, pp. 50 ff.

13   Mark O. Kistler, *Drama of the Storm & Stress* (New York, 1969), pp. 74 ff. characteristically gives his chapter on Wagner the sub-title 'A Life in the Shadow of Greatness' (p. 74).
It is in fact only in the past few years that a significant attempt has been made to establish Wagner's position as the creator of a new kind of radical dramatic realism. Of re-directive importance in this respect is the study by Johannes Werner, *Gesellschaft in literarischer Form. H.L. Wagners 'Kindermörderin' als Epochen- und Methodenparadigma* (Stuttgart, 1977). See also Huyssen, op. cit., pp. 173 ff.; Sørensen, op. cit., pp. 130 ff. References to Wagner's works are to *Sturm und Drang. Dramatische Schriften*, 2 Vols., ed. by Erich Loewenthal and Lambert Schneider (Heidelberg, N.D.) Vol. 2.

14   Kafitz, op. cit., p. 94 ff.

15   See Elise Dosenheimer, *Das deutsche soziale Drama von Lessing bis Sternheim*, (Konstanz, 1949), pp. 42 ff.

16   J.-U. Fechner discusses this and other aspects of Wagner's attempt to locate the tragic action in the city of Straßburg in his *Nachwort* to the Reclam edition of the play (Stuttgart, 1969).

Notes to chapter five

1   See Huyssen, op. cit., pp. 189 ff.

2   Hermann August Korff, Geist der Goethezeit, Vol. 1 (Leipzig, 1923), pp. 235 ff.; Kurt May, *Die Struktur des Dramas im Sturm und Drang*, in *Form und Bedeutung. Interpretationen deutscher Dichter des 18. und 19. Jahrhunderts* (Stuttgart, 1957), pp. 45-59.

3   F.J. Schneider, *Die deutsche Dichtung der Geniezeit* (Stuttgart, 1952), pp. 226 ff.; Richard Newald, *Geschichte der deutschen Literatur*, Vol. 6, 3rd. ed. (München, 1961), pp. 263 f.

4   Christoph Hering, *Friedrich Maximilian Klinger. Der Weltmann als Dichter* (Berlin, 1966), pp. 35 ff.

5   Ibid., p. 35.

6   J.P. Snapper, *The Solitary Player in Klinger's early Dramas*, Germanic Review, 45 (1970), pp. 83-93.
Karl S. Guthke, *Ferdinand Maximilian Klinger's 'Zwillinge'. Höhepunkt und Krise des Sturm und Drang*, Germanic Quarterly 43 (1970), pp. 703-714.

7 Friedrich Maximilian Klinger, *Otto* (Heilbronn, 1881) Deutsche Literatur-denkmale des 18. Jahrhunderts, Vol. 1 (Reprint Nendeln/Liechtenstein, 1968).

8 References to Klinger's plays (apart from *Otto*) are to Loewenthal and Schneider, op. cit., Vol. 2.

9 See above, pp. 95 ff.

10 Here I am in complete disagreement with the interpretation of Olga Smol-jan, *Friedrich Maximilian Klinger* (Weimar, 1962), pp. 49 ff., who attri-butes the Geheimrat's action to a class-awareness which seems to me quite alien to Klinger's conception of the figure.

11 See eg. *Otto*, pp. 102; 106 f.; *Das leidende Weib*, pp. 54 f.; 59 f.

12 Otto Ludwig, *Werke* ed. Adolf Bartels (Leipzig, N.D.) Vol. 6, pp. 212 f.

13 Huyssen, op. cit., pp. 199 ff.; Kafitz, op. cit., pp. 87 ff.

Notes to chapter six

1 Recent studies eg. by Helmuth Koopmann, *Drama der Aufklärung* (Mün-chen, 1979), pp. 134 ff. and Huyssen, op. cit., pp. 121 ff. and 202 ff.; give substantial re-statements of this view.

2 See my article *Schiller and the Drama of the Sturm und Drang*, which is due to appear shortly in *New German Studies*.

3 References are to Friedrich Schiller, *Sämtliche Werke* ed. by G. Fricke, H. G. Göpfert und H. Stubenrauch (München, 1958 f.), Vol. 1.

4 Edward McInnes, *Lessing's 'Hamburgische Dramaturgie'*, pp. 293 f.

5 Ibid., p. 295.

6 Hermann Hettner, *Das moderne Drama* (Braunschweig, 1851), p. 86.

7 Lessing, op. cit., vol. 15, p. 52.

8 See Edna Purdie, *Friedrich Hebbel* (Oxford, 1932), pp. 122 ff.

9 Edward McInnes, *Drama als Protest und Prophezeiung. Das historische Drama der Jungdeutschen*, in *Das Geschichtsdrama* ed. Elfriede Neubaur (Darmstadt, 1980), pp. 302-322.

10 Benn, op. cit., pp. 249 ff.

11 Edward McInnes, *Das deutsche Drama des 19. Jahrhunderts* (Berlin, 1983) pp. 151 ff.

12 Walter Hinck, *Produktive Rezeption heute: Am Beispiel der sozialen Dra-matik von J.M.R. Lenz & H.L. Wagner* in Hinck, *Sturm und Drang*, pp. 257-269.

SELECT BIBLIOGRAPHIE

1. Primary Sources

DIDEROT, Denis, *Oeuvres Esthétiques*, (Paris, 1959).

GOETHE, Johan Wolfgang, *Gesammelte Werke*, ed. E. Trunz (Hamburg, 1949 ff.).

HERDER, Johann Gottfried, *Sämtliche Werke*, ed. B. Suphan (Berlin, 1891).

KLINGER, Friedrich Maximilian, *Otto*, Deutsche Literaturdenkmale des 18. Jahrhunderts, ed. Bernhard Seuffert (Heilbronn, 1881). (Reprint Nendeln/ Liechtenstein, 1968).

LENZ, Jakob Michael Reinhold, *Werke und Schriften*, 2 vols., ed. Britta Titel and Helmut Haug (Stuttgart, 1966 f.).

—, *Briefe von und an J.M.R. Lenz*, ed. Karl Feye und Wolfgang Stammler (Leipzig, 1918).

LESSING, Gotthold Ephraim, *Werke*, ed. Julius Petersen and Waldemar von Olshausen (Berlin, 1925 ff.).

LOEWENTHAL, Erich and SCHNEIDER, Lambert, ed. *Sturm und Drang. Dramatische Schriften*, 2 vols. (Heidelberg, N.D.).

LUDWIG, Otto, *Werke*, ed. Adolf Bartels (Leipzig, N.D.).

MERCIER, Louis-Sébastien, *Du Théâtre. Nouvel essai sur l'art dramatique* (Amsterdam, 1773).

—, *Théâtre Complet* (Amsterdam, 1778 ff.).

NICOLAI, Heinz, ed. *Sturm und Drang. Dichtungen und theoretische Texte*, 2 vols. (München, 1971).

SCHILLER, Friedrich, *Sämtliche Werke*, ed. G. Fricke, H.G. Göpfert and H. Stubenrauch (München, 1958 f.).

2. Secondary Sources

a) Collections

GRIMMINGER, Rolf, ed. *Deutsche Aufklärung bis zur französischen Revolution 1680-1789. Hansers Sozialgeschichte der deutschen Literatur*, Vol. 3. (München, 1980).

HINCK, Walter, ed. *Sturm und Drang. Ein literaturwissenschaftliches Studienbuch* (Kronberg/Ts., 1978).

WACKER, Manfred, ed. *Sturm und Drang* (Darmstadt, 1985).

WUTHENOW, Ralph-Rainer, ed. *Zwischen Absolutismus und Aufklärung*, Vol. 4 of *Deutsche Literatur. Eine Sozialgeschichte*, ed. Horst Albert Glaser (Reinbek, 1980).

b) Single Studies

BENN, Maurice, *The Drama of Revolt. A Critical Study of Georg Büchner* (Cambridge, 1976).

BÖCKMANN, Paul, 'Der dramatische Perspektivismus in der deutschen Shakespeare-Deutung', in *Formensprache. Studien zur Literaturästhetik und Dichtungsinterpretation* (Hamburg, 1966).

BRAEMER, Edith, *Goethes 'Prometheus' und die Grundpositionen des Sturm und Drang*, 2nd ed. (Weimar, 1963).

BUTLER, Michael, 'Character and Paradox in Lenz's *Der Hofmeister*'. *German Life and Letters* 32 (1979), pp. 95-103.

DANN, Otto, 'Epoche – sozialgeschichtlicher Abriß', in Wuthenow, op. cit., pp. 12-25.

DOSENHEIMER, Elise, *Das deutsche soziale Drama von Lessing bis Sternheim* (Konstanz, 1949).

DUNCAN, Bruce, 'The Comic Structure of Lenz's *Soldaten*', *Modern Language Notes*, 91 (1976), pp. 515-523.

EIBL, Karl, *Lessing, 'Miß Sara Sampson'* (Frankfurt a.M., 1971).

FECHNER, Jörg-Ulrich, ed. *H.L. Wagner 'Die Kindermörderin'* (Stuttgart, 1969).

FRIEDRICH, Theodor, *Die Anmerkungen übers Theater des Dichters J.M.R. Lenz* (Leipzig, 1909).

FRYE, Northorp, *Anatomy of Criticism* (Princeton, 1951).

GENTON, Elisabeth, *Jakob Michael Reinhold Lenz et la Scène Allemande* (Paris, 1966).

GILLIES, Alexander, 'Herder's Essay on Shakespeare. "Das Herz der Untersuchung"', *Modern Language Review*, 32 (1937), pp. 262-280.

GIRARD, René, *Lenz 1751-1792. Genèse d'une Dramaturgie du Tragi-Comique*, (Paris, 1966).

GLASER, Horst Albert, 'Drama des Sturm und Drang', in Wuthenow, op. cit., pp. 299-322.

GRAHAM, Ilse, 'Götz von Berlichingen's Right Hand', *German Life and Letters* 16 (1963), pp. 212-228.

GRIMMINGER, Rolf, 'Aufklärung, Absolutismus und bürgerliche Individuen. Über den notwendigen Zusammenhang von Literatur, Gesellschaft und Staat in der Geschichte des 18. Jahrhunderts', in Grimminger, op. cit., pp. 15-102.

GUTHKE, Karl, S., *Das deutsche bürgerliche Trauerspiel*, 3rd ed. (Stuttgart, 1980).

—, *Geschichte und Poetik der deutschen Tragikomödie* (Göttingen, 1961).

—, 'F.M. Klingers *Zwillinge*. Höhepunkt und Krise des Sturm und Drang', *German Quarterly*, 43 (1970), pp. 703-714.

GUTHRIE, John, *Lenz & Büchner. Studies in Dramatic Form* (Frankfurt a.M., 1984).

HARRIS, Edward P., 'Structural Unity in J.M.R. Lenz's *Der Hofmeister*', *Seminar* 8, 1972, pp. 77-87.

HERING, Christoph, *Friedrich Maximilian Klinger. Der Weltmann als Dichter* (Berlin, 1966).

HETTNER, Herman, *Das moderne Drama* (Braunschweig, 1851).

HINCK, Walter, 'Produktive Rezeption heute. Am Beispiel der sozialen Dramatik von J.M.R. Lenz und H.L. Wagner', in Hinck, *Sturm und Drang*, pp. 257-269.

HUYSSEN, Andreas, *Drama des Sturm und Drang. Kommentar zu einer Epoche* (München, 1980).

INBAR, Eva Maria, *Shakespeare in Deutschland: Der Fall Lenz* (Tübingen, 1982).

ISAACSEN, Hertha, *Der junge Herder und Shakespeare* (Berlin, 1930).

KAFITZ, Dieter, *Grundzüge einer Geschichte des deutschen Dramas von Lessing bis zum Naturalismus* (Königstein/Ts., 1982).

KINDERMANN, Heinz, *Jakob Michael Reinhold Lenz und die deutsche Romantik* (Wien, 1925).

137

KISTLER, Mark O., *Drama of the Storm and Stress* (New York, 1969).

KLIEß, Werner, *Sturm und Drang* (Velbert, 1966).

KOOPMANN, Helmut, *Drama der Aufklärung. Kommentar zu einer Epoche* (München, 1979).

KORFF, Hermann August, *Geist der Goethezeit. Versuch einer ideellen Entwicklung der klassich-romantischen Literaturgeschichte*, Vol. 1, (Leipzig, 1923).

KRAFT, Herbert, *Schillers 'Kabale und Liebe'. Das Mannheimer Soufflierbuch* (Mannheim, 1963).

KREUTZER, Leo, 'Literatur als Einmischung: Jakob Michael Reinhold Lenz' in Hinck, *Sturm und Drang*, pp. 213-229.

LAMPORT, F.J., *Lessing and the Drama* (Oxford, 1981).

LUKÁCS, Georg, *Faust und Faustus. Ausgewählte Schriften* (Reinbek, 1967).

MARTINI, Fritz, 'Die feindlichen Brüder. Zum Problem des gesellschaftskritischen Dramas von J.A. Leisewitz, F.M. Klinger und F. Schiller in *Geschichte im Drama — Drama in der Geschichte* (Stuttgart, 1979), pp. 129-186.

—, 'Goethes *Götz von Berlichingen*. Charakterdrama und Gesellschaftsdrama', idem. pp. 104-128.

—, 'J.M.R. Lenz: *Anmerkungen übers Theater*', idem, pp. 80-103.

—, 'Die Poetik des Dramas im Sturm und Drang', idem. pp. 39-79.

MASON, Eudo C., *Goethe's 'Faust'. Its Genesis and Purport'* (Berkley, 1969).

MATTENKLOTT, Gert, *Melancholie in der Dramatik des Sturm und Drang* (Stuttgart, 1968).

MAY, Kurt, 'Die Struktur des Dramas im Sturm und Drang', in *Form und Bedeutung. Interpretationen deutscher Dichter des 18. und 19. Jahrhunderts* (Stuttgart, 1957), pp. 45-59.

McINNES, Edward, *Das Drama des 19. Jahrhunderts* (Berlin, 1983).

—, 'Drama als Protest und Prophezeiung. Das historische Drama der Jungdeutschen', in *Das Geschichtsdrama*, ed. Elfriede Neubaur (Darmstadt, 1980), pp. 302-322.

—, *J.M.R. Lenz. 'Die Soldaten'* (München, 1977).

—, 'Lessings *Hamburgische Dramaturgie* und die Theorie des Dramas im 19. Jahrhundert', *Orbis Litterarum*, 28 (1973), pp. 293-318.

—, 'Louis-Sébastien Mercier and the Drama of the Sturm und Drang', *Proceedings of the English Goethe Soeciety*, Vol. 54 (1984), pp. 76-100.

NÄGELE, Rainer, 'Götz von Berlichingen. Eine Geschichte und ihre Rekonstruktion' in Neue Interpretationen zu Goethes Dramen, ed. W. Hinderer (Stuttgart, 1980), pp. 65-77.

NEUHAUS, Volker, 'Götz von Berlichingen' in Geschichte als Schauspiel, ed. Walter Hinck, (Frankfurt a.M., 1981), pp. 82-100.

NEWALD, Richard, Von Klopstock bis zu Goethes Tod. 1750-1832. 1. Teil. Ende der Aufklärung und Vorbereitung der Klassik. Geschichte der deutschen Literatur von den Anfängen bis zur Gegenwart, ed. H. de Boor and R. Newald, Vol. 6/1 3rd ed. (München, 1963).

OSBORNE, John, J.M.R. Lenz. The Renunciation of Heroism (Göttingen, 1975).

PASCAL, Roy, The German Sturm und Drang (Manchester, 1953).

PURDIE, Edna, Friedrich Hebbel (Oxford, 1932).

PUSEY, W.W., Louis-Sébastien Mercier in Germany (New York, 1939).

ROBERTSON, J.G., Lessing's Dramatic Theory (Cambridge, 1939).

ROSANOW, M.N., J.M.R. Lenz, der Dichter der Sturm und Drang-Periode (Leipzig, 1909).

RYDER, Frank, 'Towards a Revaluation of Goethe's 'Götz'. The Protagonist', P.M.L.A. 77 (1962), pp. 58-70.

—, 'Towards a Revaluation of Goethe's 'Götz'. Features of Recurrence', P.M. L.A. 79 (1964), pp. 58-66.

SAUDER, Gerhard, 'Geniekult im Sturm und Drang', in Grimminger, op. cit. pp. 327-340.

SCHAER, Wolfgang, Die Gesellschaft im deutschen bürgerlichen Drama des 18. Jahrhunderts (Bonn, 1963).

SCHMIDT, Erich, Lenz und Klinger (Berlin, 1878).

SCHRIMPF, Hans-Joachim, Lessing und Brecht (Pfullingen, 1965).

SCHNEIDER, F.J., Die deutsche Dichtung der Geniezeit (Stuttgart, 1952).

SCHULTE-SASSE, Jochen, 'Drama' in Grimminger, op. cit., pp. 423-499.

—, 'Poetik und Ästhetik Lessings und seiner Zeitgenossen', idem., pp. 304-326.

SENGLE, Friedrich, Das deutsche Geschichtsdrama. Geschichte eines literarischen Mythos (Stuttgart, 1952).

SIEGRIST, Christoph, 'Aufklärung und Sturm und Drang. Gegeneinander oder Nebeneinander?', in Hinck, Sturm und Drang, pp. 1-13.

SMOLJAN, Olga, F.M. Klinger. Leben und Werk (Weimar, 1962).

139

SNAPPER, Johan Pieter, 'The Solitary Player in Klinger's Early Dramas', *Germanic Review*, 45 (1970), pp. 83-93.

SØRENSEN, Bengt Algot, *Herrschaft und Zärtlichkeit. Der Patriarchalismus und das Drama im 18. Jahrhundert* (München, 1984).

STAIGER, Emil, *Goethe*. Vol. 1, 1749-1786, 4th ed. (Zürich, 1964).

STOLPE, Heinz, *Die Auffassung des jungen Herder vom Mittelalter* (Weimar, 1955).

SZONDI, Peter, *Die Theorie des bürgerlichen Trauerspiels im 18. Jahrhundert*, ed. Gert Mattenklott (Frankfurt a.M., 1973).

WEBER, Beat, *Die Kindermörderin im deutschen Schrifttum von 1770-1795* (Bonn, 1974).

WEBER, Gottfried, *Herder und das Drama* (Weimar, 1922).

WERNER, Johannes, *Gesellschaft in literarischer Form. H.L. Wagners 'Kindermörderin' als Epochen- und Methodenparadigma* (Stuttgart, 1977).

WERTHEIM, Ursula, 'Die Helferstein-Szene in Goethes *Urgötz* und ihre Beziehungen zum Volkslied, *Weimarer Beiträge*, 1 (1955), pp. 112-143.

WIERLACHER, Alois, *Das bürgerliche Drama. Seine theoretische Begründung im 18. Jahrhundert* (München, 1968).

WIESE, Benno von, *Die deutsche Tragödie von Lessing bis Hebbel*, 2nd ed. (Hamburg, 1952).

WÖLFEL, Kurt, 'Moralische Anstalt. Zur Dramaturgie von Gottsched bis Lessing', in *Deutsche Dramentheorien*, ed. Reinhold Grimm (Frankfurt a.M., 1971), pp. 45-122.

STUDIEN ZUR DEUTSCHEN LITERATUR DES 19. UND 20. JAHRHUNDERTS

Herausgegeben von Dieter Kafitz (Mainz)

Band 1 Kafitz, Dieter (Hrsg.): Dekadenz in Deutschland. Beiträge zur Erforschung der Romanliteratur um die Jahrhundertwende. 1987.

Band 2 Thomas Fraund: Bewegung - Korrektur - Utopie. Studien zum Verhältnis von Melancholie und Ästhetik im Erzählwerk Thomas Bernhards. 1986.

Band 3 Edward McInnes: 'Ein ungeheures Theater'. The Drama of the Sturm und Drang. 1987.